KEYS TO CHILDREN'S SLEEP PROBLEMS

Susan E. Gottlieb, M.D.

D1602729

BARRON'S

Cover photo by Scott Barrow, Inc., Cold Spring, NY

DEDICATION

To my husband, Matt Greenberg, for his love and support; my mother, Justine Gottlieb, for a world of possibilities; and my daughter, Ali Greenberg, for all the practical experience.

All inquiries should be addressed to:
Barron's Educational Series, Inc.
250 Wireless Boulevard
Hauppauge, NY 11788

Library of Congress Catalog Card No. 92-36445

International Standard Book No. 0-8120-4940-3

Library of Congress Cataloging-in-Publication Data

Gottlieb, Susan E.
  Keys to children's sleep problems / Susan E. Gottlieb.
    p. cm. — (Barron's parenting keys)
  Includes index.
  ISBN 0-8120-4940-3
    1. Sleep disorders in children.   2. Children—Sleep.   I.
Title. II. Series.
RJ506.S55G68   1993
618.92′8498–dc20
                                           92-36445
                                           CIP

PRINTED IN THE UNITED STATES OF AMERICA

3456 5500 987654321

CONTENTS

INTRODUCTION

Bedtime can either be a warm and cozy time for family togetherness, or it can be the most dreaded part of the day. This book is designed to help parents understand children's sleep and enable them to manage common sleep problems.

The first step is to understand normal sleep patterns. The chapters comprising Part One trace the development of sleep behavior from infancy through school age. Each chapter highlights milestones in children's motor, language, and thinking abilities that can also affect sleep. Common age-related sleep difficulties are described so that parents are able to anticipate and plan for them.

The best approach to sleep problems is prevention. This is the focus of Part Two, Building Good Sleep Habits. This section emphasizes how to organize a daily schedule, recognize fatigue, and set up a bedroom that promotes sleep. Parents discover the benefits of a bedtime ritual and have an opportunity to review some of the most creative. Naps, temperament, sleeping through the night, and co-sleeping are among the other topics considered.

Sleep problems are common during childhood. Few children grow up without experiencing them. The range of problems is immense. Some children find it hard to settle down at bedtime. Others fall asleep quickly but wake up numerous times during the night. There are children who sleep well but rise, ready to start the day, at dawn. Bad dreams and nighttime fears are universal phenomena. Sleep can be affected by colic, night feedings, or illness.

Parents do not have to stand by and wait for these problems to disappear on their own. In Part Three, Dealing with Sleep Problems, parents can learn about the causes and management of sleep problems by following actual case studies from initial presentation to final resolution. Insights gained in this section allow parents to approach their children's sleep problems with empathy, confidence, and understanding. It is stressful to live with a child who is not sleeping well. This is why Part Three also includes a chapter with hints on how parents can cope until the sleep problem is solved.

Sleep disorders are the subject of Part Four. Sleep disorders are distinguished from sleep problems by having their origins in the actual structure or quality of the sleep itself. Insomnia, night terrors, sleepwalking, sleeptalking, bedwetting, and sleep apnea are the conditions covered in Part Four. Descriptions of these conditions and their treatment are, again, presented in a detailed case study format.

The last part of the book contains a question-and-answer section, a glossary of technical terms, and a resource listing of helpful organizations, books, tapes, and other devices.

The effort involved in preventing or working on sleep problems can be enormous. However, the outcome—happier and more energetic parents and children—is truly worthwhile.

Part One

NORMAL SLEEP PATTERNS

1

INFANT SLEEP

The first year of life is a time of remarkable developments: a baby triples her birth weight, learns the fundamentals of walking and talking, and establishes relationships with the central people in her life. Dramatic changes in a baby's capacity to organize sleep and wakefulness mirror the advances in these other domains. This chapter describes the links between developmental and sleep milestones. Infancy is also the time to launch good sleep habits. Good sleep habits are the key to preventing many of the common sleep problems of childhood.

The First Quarter: 0 to 3 Months

The baby's task during the first quarter of the first year is to adjust to life outside the womb. Meeting the baby's needs promptly and consistently is critical to a successful transition.

A baby is equipped, from the start, with a behavioral repertoire that enables her to communicate her needs. The parents, for their part, learn to read their baby's behavioral signals so that they can provide appropriate care. For instance, Miriam is crying loudly, sucking vigorously on her fist, and hasn't eaten in two hours. Her parents make these observations, conclude that she must be hungry, and offer her food.

Parents can also learn to recognize sleep-related behavior patterns. If the parents set the stage for sleep at appropriate times, then the baby can start to establish regular sleep habits. A baby who has a regular sleep pattern sleeps more at night, is awake longer during the day, and takes solid daytime naps rather than frequent catnaps.

During the first three months of life, a baby sleeps 16 to 17 hours per day. Periods of sleep and wakefulness are evenly distributed throughout the 24-hour day. The usual pattern is 3 hours of sleep followed by 1 hour of alertness. This pattern is directly related to the feeding cycle. When a baby is satiated, she falls asleep. She awakens again when she is hungry and stays awake for a short time after the feeding. At this age, a baby cannot keep herself awake.

Parents can take advantage of this natural cycle when trying to set regular sleep patterns. After the baby has been up for an hour, parents should try to encourage sleep. This can be accomplished by toning down the level of stimulation or moving to a dark and quiet room. It helps the baby's organization if she sleeps in a consistent place. She eventually comes to associate this place with sleep. The baby's room does not have to be soundproofed. Parents need not worry about the telephone ringing or other children playing nearby. A baby has an innate ability to shut out interfering stimuli when she needs to sleep.

By about six weeks, the infant begins to demonstrate one daily period of sustained alertness, which usually occurs in the afternoon. This is an ideal time to take the baby outside. Providing stimulation when the baby is awake heightens the contrast between sleeping and waking and promotes a more regular daily routine.

Toward the end of this 3-month period, a new pattern starts to emerge. Parents may notice that the baby always becomes drowsy in the morning and early afternoon. This is the beginning of the two-nap pattern that is usually maintained up to 12 months of age. To encourage this pattern, parents should try to arrange their daily schedules so that they are home during these drowsy periods. Sleep comes more easily in a familiar environment.

Babies who were born prematurely have a somewhat different pattern. Initially, they tend to be sleepier than full-term infants. They then show an increased level of alertness around the time that they were expected to be born.

The Second Quarter: 3 to 6 Months

The three to six month old seems vastly different from an infant only a few months younger. She seems much more predictable, understandable, and responsive. Her newly developed skills of reaching for and manipulating objects, laughing, cooing, and imitating sounds enable her to act as a social partner.

The baby's schedule at this age is far more socially acceptable as well. She sleeps about 14 hours in total: 9 to 10 hours at night and 4 to 5 hours during the day. The day usually begins between 6 and 8 A.M. She takes two or three naps per day at relatively consistent times. Bedtime is between 7 and 9 P.M. Another major advance is that 50 to 70 percent of infants in this age group sleep seven hours in a row at night.

The sleep schedule must still accommodate her feeding needs. Some babies at this age continue to require a feeding at night. This usually takes place four to six hours after the last feeding. Other babies are hungry in the early morning. If a late night or early morning feeding is given, it is important that it be done without overstimulation. This way the baby does not confuse these times with playtime.

The Third Quarter: 6 to 9 Months

Between six and nine months, a baby makes several critical developmental advances. There is a spurt in large

4

muscle activity as she begins to sit, crawl, and pull up to a standing position. The development of fine motor skills allows a baby of this age to pick up small objects. Eye-hand coordination also improves.

The infant's thinking capacity is propelled by the understanding of *object permanence*. A baby starts to realize that people and objects continue to exist even when they are not currently in view. A baby explores this concept by playing games like peekaboo and hide-and-seek. These games are very reassuring because the object that has disappeared always returns. A baby also learns to distinguish familiar people from people seen only infrequently. This phenomenon is *stranger awareness.*

The daily schedule becomes even more refined. Feedings number three to six per day. Total sleep per day ranges between 13 and 15 hours. A typical schedule includes wake-up at 6:30 A.M., two naps at 9 to 10:30 A.M. and 1:30 to 3 P.M., and bedtime at 7:30 P.M. Of all infants, 60 to 80 percent sleep through the night. The link between sleep and feeding has lessened. A baby does not regularly drop off to sleep after meals if she is provided with sufficiently stimulating activities.

This is a good age to establish a bedtime ritual if it has not evolved on its own. The bedtime ritual provides a soothing transition from activity to sleep. It often starts with a bath and may incorporate reading, singing, or cuddling. A critical element is the finale. The baby should be set down awake in the place where she is expected to spend the night. Once she learns how to fall asleep on her own there, she is able to handle any nighttime wakings in a similar fashion.

The study of object permanence takes place at nighttime as well as during the day. A resurgence in night crying

5

is noted in this age group, even among infants who previously slept through the night without difficulty. This phenomenon is *developmental night crying*. The infant has a normal waking after light sleep and finds herself alone. She is now aware that her parents are out there somewhere, and she cries as a way of bringing them back.

It is important for the parents to offer reassurance to the infant at this time. She needs to know that her parents will return to her. Parents should provide comfort without introducing complicating factors, such as feeding, playing, or removing her from the crib. The less stimulating the interaction, the more quickly can the infant return to sleep. Talking in a calm voice, patting her on the back, or turning on the music box are maneuvers that soothe the baby. Repeating some of the components of the bedtime ritual may also be effective in reorienting the infant to sleep. Developmental night crying stops on its own once the baby has a firm grasp of object permanence.

Parents may also encourage the infant to go to sleep with a special object, such as a cuddly toy or soft blanket. This *transitional object* provides a physical link between the waking and sleeping states. Not all infants form such an attachment. If an infant does, tucking in the toy or making sure that she has the blanket in hand becomes an important element of the bedtime ritual.

If an infant is struggling with object permanence, it can be helpful to give her something to sleep with that belongs to a parent.This may be a shirt or scarf that she has seen the parent wear and that still bears the parent's scent. The infant knows that the parent will come back for the item and is comforted by having a "piece" of the parent to take to bed with her.

6

The Fourth Quarter: 9 to 12 Months

The last quarter of the first year marks the start of the quest for independence. The infant who crawls or walks can regulate the physical distance between herself and her caretakers. Words and gestures enable her to make demands on the environment. The infant is, in turn, thrilled and terrified by these powerful new skills.

By this age, the infant sleeps 14 hours per day; 12 of these hours are at night, with two hourlong daily naps. A typical day begins at 6:30 or 7:00 A.M., includes naps at 10 A.M. and 1 P.M., and ends at a 7 P.M. bedtime. Some infants give up the morning nap at around the time of the first birthday. They adjust by taking a long nap after lunch or taking a short nap and going to bed earlier.

The infant's prodigious physical activity has implications for sleep behavior. An infant who practices walking all day may have increased sleep needs. Some babies even practice pulling up to a stand and walking in the crib. They may cry for help at night when they discover that, although they can pull themselves up, they do not know how to get down. This is a skill that needs to be worked on during the daytime.

The sleep ritual may need to be longer to allow the infant sufficient time to settle down. Parents should count on spending at least 20 minutes in transition time.

New habits, such as finger sucking and headbanging, emerge at this time. Various explanations have been offered to account for this finding. One theory is that these behaviors serve as comforting maneuvers for the infant. Another is that they are outlets for excess energy.

Another development is resistance to going to bed. This is the first time that the infant actually has the

7

physical capacity to keep herself awake. She might choose to exercise this new ability because of tension, a reluctance to be separated from people to whom she has become particularly attached, or an unwillingness to leave the excitement of daily life.

Sleep Problems in the First Year

The infant makes dramatic changes in sleep behavior over the first year of life. Habits formed during this time can also be the basis for sleep problems.

The most vexing problem in the first year is failure to sleep through the night. An infant may wake at night because she is used to being played with or fed. She may lack the ability to settle herself back down after a normal night awakening. A small percentage of infants lack the physiological maturity to sleep through the night. There is no evidence that feeding practices, such as giving the baby cereal at night, influence the age at which she starts to sleep through the night. Sleeping through the night is explained in greater detail in Key 10.

A decision about the family bed should also be made within the first year of life. An infant can easily adjust to sleeping by herself or sleeping with her parents. Once sleep habits are formed, however, making changes is more complicated. This topic is covered in Key 12.

An infant may sleep well but at the wrong time of day. Parents can remedy this by emphasizing the differences between daytime and nighttime caretaking. Nighttime interactions should be low-key, businesslike, and boring. Parents should provide the infant with plenty of stimulation when she is awake during the day.

If parents want the infant to reserve the bulk of her sleep for the night, then daytime sleep must be limited. If the baby is sleeping for a 5-hour stretch during the day, this time can be gradually pared down by ½-hour intervals until it reaches an appropriate nap length for the baby's age. A sleep ritual also works to convey the message of bedtime.

Infancy is an exciting time that can really be enjoyed if all family members are well rested.

2

TODDLER SLEEP

Two-year-old Flavia climbed to the top of the step stool for the first time. From her high perch, she enjoyed a new perspective on the living room. "Look at me!" she crowed. Mrs. Todaro applauded her daughter's achievement. Flavia beamed. Then, Flavia saw a toy she wanted and began to climb down the ladder. She dangled one foot, but the steps that were so easy to climb now seemed perilously far apart. She turned and attempted to climb down backward, but she could still not lower herself enough to reach the step. She began to pound her fists on the railing and cry bitterly. Mrs. Todaro scooped up Flavia and stroked her back until the tears subsided.

Life with a one to three year old is a roller coaster ride. At one moment, she relentlessly pursues autonomy. "Me do it" becomes her favorite phrase. All of a toddler's new skills—walking, running, talking, self-feeding, dressing, and using the toilet—allow her greater independence than she has ever experienced before. She can regulate the distance between herself and her caretaker. She can express her ideas, issue commands, and ask questions. She has more control over her body and requires less assistance from adults to perform activities of daily living.

It is exhilarating to climb to the top of the ladder, but it is devastating when the skills needed to climb down are

10

lacking. When her new abilities disappoint, the toddler seeks solace in the parent's arms.

The toddler plunges eagerly into activities without thinking ahead. Sometimes this results in elation, other times in frustration. Toddlerhood involves a growing recognition of limits. The toddler is affected by externally imposed parental rules as well as by the physical limitations of her own body. A toddler also learns that independence cannot be achieved without separation.

Living with a toddler requires patience, flexibility, diplomacy, and humor. The parent's role is to structure safe contexts for the exercise of autonomy. A parent must guide without smothering and provide freedom without chaos.

Sleep Schedules

Toddlers can be expected to sleep between 12 and 13½ hours per day. An hour or two of this time is usually spent napping. Naptimes can range widely with some toddlers sleeping for 20 minutes and others sleeping 4 hours.

At the beginning of the toddler period, there may be two daily naps. A typical schedule includes waking at 6:30 A.M., a 1-½-hour nap at 9:30 A.M., another nap from 2 to 3:30 P.M., and bedtime at 7 P.M. By 15 to 18 months, toddlers enter a transition phase: two naps are too much and one nap is not enough. Bedtime may have to be moved up temporarily to compensate.

Most toddlers have reached the one nap a day stage by two years. The ideal schedule situates this nap after lunch. An early afternoon nap gives children enough energy to get them pleasantly through the day without interfering with a reasonable bedtime.

Sometimes a parent must put an end to an overly long nap. This must be done with extreme gentleness. A parent should count on at least 30 minutes before the child is truly ready to resume full activity.

Parents should also be aware of the ways in which toddlers show they are overtired. Their physical coordination is affected, perhaps with a lessening of manual dexterity and more frequent falls. They are more easily frustrated and can be provoked to tears over a trivial incident. Children may not nap at these times, but parents can certainly encourage them to rest. Parents can ensure that their children rest by engaging in quiet activities with them.

Toddler Sleep Problems

Control and separation figure prominently in toddler sleep problems. Bedtime resistance is seen in over 50 percent of toddlers, because bedtime represents the ultimate separation.

Toddlers worry that the configuration of their precious world will change while they are asleep. This is true even if they live in an extremely stable environment. Toddlers' limited thinking capacities prevent them from applying what they've learned in the past to future events. Going to bed each night is a leap of faith.

Toddlers don't want to leave the daytime world, scene of triumph and achievement. Toddlers do not want to be excluded from any fascinating activities in the household. Toddlers are also sensitive to ultimatums. They do not like being ordered to bed. Part of defining themselves means taking a different viewpoint from their parents. If they sense that going to bed is very important to the parents, they oppose this idea on toddler principle.

A common manifestation of bedtime resistance is the curtain call syndrome (see Key 20). The child calls or leaves bed repeatedly with a variety of requests. These requests are a tactic used to delay bedtime and the separation that accompanies it. If the parents respond, the child is encouraged and the behavior continues. Resolving this problem requires the parents to set and adhere to consistent limits.

Another common toddler sleep problem is frequent night wakings. These usually occur when a toddler has not learned how to put herself back to sleep after a normal spontaneous waking at night. This may be a child who is used to falling asleep while being rocked or sucking on a bottle. A child needs a self-sufficient routine for getting to sleep so that she can re-create these phenomena when she wakes at night. Altering the child's sleep onset associations alleviates this problem. A method for accomplishing this is described in Key 16.

A toddler who sleeps in a bed has nighttime mobility. Parents need to decide how they will handle nocturnal visits. Responses range from welcoming the child into their bed, to setting up a sleeping bag on the floor, to returning the child promptly to her bed as soon as her presence is noted. Whatever they decide, parents must present firm and consistent rules to the toddler. More discussion on this topic can be found in Key 22.

Toddlers can experience nightmares, usually related to stresses in the child's daily life. If a toddler is having frequent nightmares, it is advisable to consider possible daytime pressures. Beginning toilet training, a new daycare situation, or a change in the family constellation might be upsetting to the child. (See also Key 24.)

Night terrors can also occur in the toddler age group. During a night terror, the child is found sitting bolt upright in bed, scared and unresponsive. The child appears to be

13

awake, but she is actually asleep and will have no memory of the event in the morning. Night terrors are a normal occurrence caused by partial awakening from deep sleep. (See also Key 27.)

The toddler's luxuriant imagination leads to fears that are expressed at bedtime. The most common fear involves separation from loved ones. Hints about dealing with children's fears are contained in Key 23.

The toddler's eagerness to start the day can be responsible for her being an early riser. Various approaches to this situation are presented in Key 21.

Preventing Toddler Sleep Problems

A good bedtime ritual can appease some of the toddler's bedtime resistance. It provides time for the toddler to adjust to the idea of the nightly separation. If the ritual is fun, the child participates eagerly. If it is effective, the child is lulled to sleep by its conclusion.

The bedtime ritual is the perfect model of autonomy under controlled conditions. The parents should designate how many books will be read, but the toddler can select the specific titles. The child can also choose between the purple pajamas and the pink nightgown. If only one tape is to be played, let the child decide whether it is Raffi or reggae. The ritual should conclude with a comforting reminder of parental constancy, such as "See you in the morning."

The ritual also appeals to a toddler's penchant for control. Once a format is in place, it is immensely comforting to the child to be able to anticipate in each step in the process. She insists that it proceed every night in the same way. Further information about bedtime rituals is contained in Keys 6 and 7.

14

The toddler still takes a special object to bed with her. This comfort object provides a physical link between waking and sleeping and therefore eases the process of transition from one state to another. The child who is not attached to a particular object can make a nightly ceremony of selecting the toy that will have the honor of keeping her company that evening.

The toddler years are a challenge to a parent's inventiveness and equilibrium. It is also a time to reexperience the many wonders of the world and the sheer joy of being alive.

3

PRESCHOOLERS AND SLEEP

Three, four, and five year olds apply their greatly elaborated language and motor skills to the wider world outside the immediate family. Their increased competence allows them a greater degree of control over their environment.

Preschoolers have the motor command that enables them to run, jump, and climb with ease. Their fine motor skills allow them to build with blocks, manipulate scissors, and control a pencil or paintbrush.

Language capabilities expand as well. Their vocabulary is now measured in thousands of words. Sentences increase in length and grammatical complexity. They ask questions—around 400 a day. They are better able to understand concepts like being tired, hungry, or cold. They can listen to explanations and supply relevant answers when asked a question. Their speech is intelligible not only to close family members but to all adults.

Preschoolers' thinking has been described as egocentric. They watch the moon move in the sky and believe that it is following them. Their acceptance of animism motivates them, after a fall, to hit the "bad sidewalk" that injured them. Preschool children still have difficulty understanding that others may not always share their viewpoint.

Children strive to establish a sense of self during this period. They develop a strong gender identity and an identification with the parent of the same sex.

Children at this age continue to explore the concept of control but in a more sophisticated way than toddlers. They still need their parents to establish firm and consistent limits for behavior. Preschoolers are quite adept at recognizing inconsistencies. If they sense ambivalence, they begin an aggressive campaign of bargaining and manipulation. This is a good time to introduce the concept of actions and their consequences. Although cause and effect may not be completely understood by the young preschooler, it will be a clear idea by the end of this period.

Preschoolers have wonderful imaginations and can engage in true collaborative play with peers. They enjoy dramatic play in which they reenact aspects of their lives or favorite stories.

Marvelous imaginations can also create things to fear. Preschoolers fear noisy, violent, uncontrolled entities. Fears may also involve animals and imaginary creatures. These extrinsic targets reflect the inner struggle that preschoolers experience. Preschoolers are attempting to control powerful sexual and aggressive feelings and worry about not being able to contain them. Additional fears are created by preschoolers' tendencies to attribute human qualities to inanimate objects.

Preschool Sleep Schedules

All these developments have relevance for sleep behavior. Preschoolers sleep 11 to 12 hours per night. Most have given up the afternoon nap. Napping is something they associate with babies, and preschoolers certainly want to distinguish themselves from babies. Particularly after a hectic day at school, though, children aged three, four, and five may be tired in the late afternoon.

17

Parents should attempt to provide some time for reenergizing in the afternoon. Children accept a slowdown in activities provided it is not called nap or rest time. An effective slowdown strategy is the "video nap." During a video nap, the children are given the opportunity to watch a short, nonviolent video tape. They may fall asleep as they watch the tape. Compliance is enhanced if the parent stays in the room—viewing the tape, reading a magazine, or doing some paperwork. This way, the children are not tormented with curiosity about what other, potentially more exciting activities, are going on elsewhere in the house. Even if the children do not fall asleep, they will have shared some quiet time with the parent.

There are other variations on the slowdown strategy. Special toys, such as blackboards, puzzles, and small figures, can be set aside for play only at this designated time. This is also an excellent time for books. Some children want to page through the books themselves or pretend to read to an audience of stuffed animals. Others enjoy being read to or following along with a book on tape.

Preschool Sleep Problems

A commonly encountered sleep problem at this age is bedtime resistance. Preschoolers can be endlessly inventive about why they cannot possibly get to sleep. This is a time when parents must set and stick to firm limits regarding bedtime.

Preschoolers can understand that a certain hour is their bedtime. They can even be taught the configuration on the clock that corresponds to this time. They can be reminded, in a concrete way about how much playtime remains by using a timer. Once the timer rings, they must stop playing and get ready for bed. The timer is much more objective than a parent and is indifferent to the pleas of "just five more minutes."

18

Parents can use the childrens' desires for control and praise to foster compliance. Instead of arguing about the childrens' delaying tactics, they can offer a prize for getting into bed on time. A sticker can be placed on the calendar for each fuss-free night. Several stickers in a row might translate into a special reward on the weekend.

Various anxieties of preschoolers can lead to sleep disturbances. Recognition and response by the parents can frequently assist preschoolers in overcoming their anxieties. Fortunately for parents, preschool children are usually articulate enough to reveal what is troubling them.

Common anxieties include fear of wetting the bed at night, school-related stress, and concerns about hospitalization and death. Bedwetting is still quite common and normal at this age. The child who is afraid he will wet the bed might be relieved to wear diapers or disposable training pants at night for awhile longer, provided the parents or siblings do not tease him or make him feel like a baby. If a child voices concern about school, a parents' conference with the teacher may prove enlightening. Nighttime problems can be expected in a child who was hospitalized for up to six weeks following discharge. The parents need to reassure the child, in developmentally appropriate language, about what is being done to keep him healthy.

Preschoolers are also concerned about death. Parents need to explore the concept of death with their children and provide them with accurate information. After a death in the family, children typically worry that it was their fault or that their parents will die soon.

Some of these topics can be addressed using children's books. Books provide various models of coping with problems. Reading about another child's fears, for instance, can serve as a jumping-off point for a discussion of the

19

child's own fears or the fears that a parent had at that age. A list of books pertaining to fears is included at the end of this book.

The preschool age is a peak time for nightmares. A nightmare is evidence that a child is actively and very appropriately working through his life experiences. Nightmares are usually populated by animals or scary imaginary creatures. Common story lines involve a child who is lost or being chased. A child who has had a nightmare needs reassurance and empathy. He may feel better to be reminded that a dream is just a story inside his head. It is important, however, not to belittle the very real feelings that the nightmare engenders. Occasional nightmares are not a cause for concern. Frequent nightmares, with a recurring theme, require further investigation to uncover the source of the child's fears and help him find additional ways to deal with them. (See Key 23 for a fuller discussion.)

Preschool children may also voice fears before going to bed. They may complain of creatures under the bed or outside the window. Children need to be reassured that the parents are available to protect them. A positive bedtime ritual that provides soothing images before sleep may be helpful. (See Keys 6, 7, and 23.)

The preschool years are a delightful time. Good sleep habits ensure that these years are enjoyed by all family members.

4

~~~~~~

SLEEP AND SCHOOL-AGED CHILDREN

T he focus of middle childhood, ages 6 through 10, is on competence and productivity as an individual and as a member of a family, a school, and a community.

Self-esteem becomes a major preoccupation at this age. Self-esteem can derive from a child's achievements in school or in a sport or hobby. Acceptance by peers can also lead to enhanced self-esteem. A child can gain a sense of self-esteem by planning his own activities, managing his own schedule, carrying out chores at home, or handling an allowance. Positive feedback from the successful completion of these tasks leads to increased enthusiasm for future tasks. Inadequate performance gives a child a sense of inferiority.

This is an age when role models assume great importance. The role model is a competent and powerful figure, whether a real sports superstar or an imaginary television character. The role model may engage in aggressive or sexual behavior that would be totally inappropriate for a school-aged child. Through identification with such a figure, the child finds an acceptable way of channeling his own sexual and aggressive feelings. The role model's publicized achievements may serve as another motivator for the child's own productivity.

A child of this age is concerned about his body. He will be especially concerned if his body appears or functions differently from those of his friends. A child who is obese, clumsy, or wets the bed may isolate himself from others rather than risk the ridicule of his peers. Concerns about the body also bring an upsurge of somatic complaints about headaches and pains in the chest, abdomen, and limbs. These problems should be promptly addressed by a thorough pediatric evaluation.

Middle childhood brings major advances in a child's ability to think and make moral judgments. A child at this age has a better command of logic. He can focus on multiple aspects of a problem simultaneously and can solve problems mentally rather than relying on manipulation. He develops a conscience and begins to consider the person's intent when judging another's behavior.

The demands of the school environment burgeon in response to these new capacities. A child is expected to do more work. New emphasis is placed on the skills of memory, problem solving, reasoning, selective attention, and reflection.

The widening of the child's physical world, thinking ability, and imagination brings an increase in things to worry about. A child worries about bodily mutilation, being teased, academic failure, and catastrophes befalling close friends and family. News reports expose a child to epidemics, violence, and destruction.

Sleep Schedules
The challenges of middle childhood are also felt in the sleep domain. A child sleeps between 10 and 11 hours per night. The particular hours a child sleeps now are dictated by his school schedule rather than by his temperament. For a child who is a natural night owl, this can present a problem.

A recent survey of healthy 8, 9, and 10 year olds reported that 24 percent slept poorly. Almost half reported sleep difficulties that had been present for longer than six months. Some of the children were even being given sedatives to induce sleep.

Sleep Problems During Middle Childhood

The most prominent sleep problem in this age group is *insomnia*, an inability to fall asleep or stay asleep. A child with insomnia gets an inadequate amount of sleep. Insomnia in this age group is often linked to fears, stress, and worries.

The fears are much more reality based than those of preschoolers. School-aged children know that there are no monsters under the bed, but they obsess about rare circumstances under which harm might befall their loved ones. When the parents are out at night, the children worry that the parents will be involved in an avalanche, a car accident, or a bridge collapse. These children cannot sleep until their parents return home safely. This situation is exacerbated in families in which a parent travels frequently on business.

Nightmares are encountered in middle childhood. Nightmares can be a way of working through normal aggressive feelings. Nightmares can also result from exposure to scary material in movies or on television. When children spend more time away from home with friends, parents cannot monitor their television exposure as closely. They may have access to shows in other people's homes that they would not be permitted to see in their own. Parents may want to check what the children propose to watch at a friend's house. In the company of friends, children may be pressured to watch shows that they would not ordinarily choose. Parents should be alert for a resurgence of nightmares following a sleep-over. An effort should be made to learn what kind of entertainment was provided. This is an opportune time to discuss resisting peer pressure and to brainstorm about ways of handling such a situation should it arise again.

Night terrors can occur in school-aged children. They usually occur in model children who are competent and never a problem. These children often have a hard time expressing negative feelings. These feelings can eventually surface as night terrors. Night terrors in school-aged children cannot simply be dismissed as a developmental phenomenon as they were in the younger age groups. They are a distress signal and merit investigation and treatment. More information about nightmares and night terrors can be found in Table 4.1 and in Keys 24 and 27.

Table 4.1
NIGHTMARES VERSUS NIGHT TERRORS

Nightmare	Night Terror
Occurs during the last part of the night.	Occurs during the first third of the night.
Occurs during REM (rapid eye movement) sleep.	Occurs during stage 3 to 4 non-REM sleep.
Child appears frightened and is crying.	Child appears frightened or confused, with fast heart rate, sweating, bulging eyes, moaning, thrashing.
Child is easily aroused and comforted.	Child is difficult to arouse, not able to be comforted.
Child may be reluctant to go back to sleep.	Child drifts back to sleep on his own.
Child can recall a dream.	There is no dreaming.
Child can recall the event in the morning.	There is no memory of the incident in the morning.

Children who report taking longer than 30 minutes to fall asleep also report more sleepwalking and sleeptalking incidents. Children in this age group who sleepwalk, unless it occurs very infrequently, should be examined carefully by a physician.

School-aged children may be on chronic medications, such as methylphenidate (Ritalin) for attention deficit hyperactivity disorder or theophylline preparations for asthma. These medications can interfere with sleep. Sleep problems in children on these or other medications should be brought to the attention of the treating physician. A modification in the type of drug or dosing schedule may be all that is necessary to alleviate this problem.

Sleep problems in middle childhood are closely linked to the developmental advancements taking place. Sleep problems have the potential to interfere with important factors, such as self-esteem and school performance. Prompt professional attention can help a child deal with sleep problems and allow him to make the most out of an exciting and productive time in his life.

Part Two

~~~~~~

BUILDING GOOD SLEEP HABITS

5

~~~~~~

BEDTIME

Once a child understands the usual flow of events in the household, transitions are much easier. Carol, aged four, knew and expected that bedtime followed her bath and evening snack. Anticipating this, she was able to mentally prepare and pace herself. She would often announce which book she wanted to have read to her or what game she wanted to play. This was as natural a part of her day as getting up and getting dressed in the morning. As she took more responsibility for getting herself ready for bed, her parents did not have to hover and nag her.

As a result, Carol felt proud of her abilities and very competent. Carol's parents praised her, and the entire family was therefore able to approach bedtime in a warm and relaxed manner.

Mike, a six year old who did not have a specific bedtime, was deprived of this opportunity to exercise control and gain positive attention from his parents. After dinner he never knew whether to bother starting a new painting or becoming involved in block building, for fear that the activity would be interrupted before completion by the dreaded call, "Bedtime!" Much of his evening was spent aimlessly wandering around the house annoying his parents, who were desperately trying to finish their after-dinner coffee.

When his parents were ready to put him to bed, Mike had no time to prepare and reacted, appropriately, with a vigorous protest. Since he never had any opportunity to anticipate events, the call for bed seemed very arbitrary and unfair. This same battle was repeated on a nightly basis.

C hildren need structure in their lives. Every day there are new experiences to absorb, new challenges to master, and new skills to learn. Minds and bodies grow increasingly competent. In addition, children sense that other people's expectations of them rise, and they also start to expect more of themselves. To counterbalance the part of their world that is in flux, children need anchors.

A consistent daily schedule provides a much-needed sense of security in this heady and exciting time, and a regular bedtime becomes an important part of this daily routine.

Deciding a Bedtime

In deciding on a bedtime, the family's schedule and the amount of sleep that the child needs (see Table 5.1) must be taken into consideration. Transition time is also an important factor. Some active children require almost an hour to relax before they are able to fall asleep. Other children can fall asleep immediately once their heads touch the pillow.

If a child goes to school, to a sitter, or to day care in the morning, the family needs to plan a bedtime that will provide adequate sleep before wake-up time, and that will still allow sufficient time to prepare for the day's activities in the morning.

Table 5.1
AVERAGE SLEEP TIMES FOR NORMAL CHILDREN IN
FAMILIAR SURROUNDINGS

Age	Total (Hours)	Night (Hours)	Naps
1 week	16½–18		
6 months	14	11	2
1 year	13¾	11½	1–2
2 years	12–13	10½–11½	1
3 years	11–12	10–11	1
4 years	10–11½		0
5–12 years	9½–11		0

Behavioral observation is helpful in setting an appropriate bedtime. The child's behavior can be charted for several days and analyzed with respect to total amount of sleep and periods of activity and inactivity. This is especially useful as one tries to get a handle on an infant's daily schedule. Sleep times determined in conjunction with the child's own biological rhythms are accepted much more easily.

Certain behavioral cues indicate fatigue in the child. An infant may exhibit irritability, restlessness, and pallor when tired. In an older child, such habit patterns as thumb sucking, hair twirling, and eye rubbing are manifestations of fatigue. Poor coordination, frenetic activity, irritability, and even changes in voice quality can be seen. These behaviors can be used to plan and modify a child's bedtime. If they are observed before the child's usual bedtime, this is an indication that bedtime should be moved up for that particular night. Ideally, the process of going to bed should be underway before these behaviors are full-blown because of the difficulties in handling the overtired child.

Parents who have had problems with their children's sleep patterns are often advised to deprive the children of naps or exercise them vigorously before bedtime in the hope of making them sleep better. These practices will only result in an irritable child and an even more irritable adult. An overtired child is so wound up that he finds it difficult to relax sufficiently to fall asleep. The quality of his sleep is affected as well. These children are more subject to frequent awakenings at night and have an increased likelihood of experiencing night terrors. (See Key 27.)

An easier transition to sleep can be achieved if the period after dinner is designated as quiet time. This is a time to wind down from the active pace of the day. It is not the time to run out to the store to complete a last-minute errand or to start a fascinating new project. These very exciting activities make it impossible for a child to relax.

Working families must be mindful of the temptation to pack a whole day's worth of activity into the few hours between dinner and bedtime. Rather than overstimulating the child at bedtime, some parents choose to get up early and spend special time with the child in the morning.

The Role of Naps

Another influence on bedtime is the number and timing of daily naps. Naps must be counted when the child's daily sleep quotient is tallied. The more the child sleeps during the day, the less she can be expected to sleep at night.

Timing is also important. Generally speaking, a child is not ready to go to sleep for the night unless at least four hours have elapsed since his last nap. A true bedtime wrecker is the 5 P.M. nap. This can be seen in four and five year olds who come home tired after an active day in preschool. It can also occur when infants take a long or late afternoon nap. At first, this seems like a boon to a parent, who would like to use the time to unwind, prepare dinner, or make a phone call in peace. It is recognized as a true problem when nine o'clock rolls around and the child is still going strong.

Parents have several options in this situation. There are instances when the parent recognizes that the child really needs this sleep and can accommodate a later bedtime. If this occurs on a chronic basis, however, it may be an indication that the child is not getting sufficient sleep at night to carry him through the day. Instead of this nap, the family may schedule an earlier bedtime. Special distractions are then needed to prevent the child from falling asleep in the late afternoon. An effective strategy is to move up the time of the child's bath. Most children love their baths and the water play soothes and calms even the most irritable child. Dancing to soft music and blowing bubbles are other fun ways to fend off the five o'clock fusses.

Exceptions to the Rule
There will undoubtedly be exceptions to the bedtime rule for special occasions. It's almost impossible for an excited young child to go to bed when the house is filled with guests. Parents may choose to let a child stay up late to watch the fireworks on New Year's Eve or enjoy the company of friends or relatives who visit infrequently. Some children yearn to stay up all night just to see what it's like. Parents may also be more flexible about bedtime on weekends and during school vacations.

It is important when an exception is being made to state the reason for it clearly and explicitly to the child. This step is critical in dealing with future recriminations when bedtime returns to its usual hour. The sleep loss can be compensated by a nap, quiet playtime, or an earlier bedtime on the following day. Some children make up the sleep deficit by sleeping an hour or so longer for several nights in succession.

Working families sometimes find a later bedtime convenient so that the child has an opportunity to interact with the parents during the evening hours. If the child is able to sleep late in the morning, this is rarely a problem. It does prove complicated, however, if staying up later in the evening prevents the child from getting an adequate amount of sleep.

Sleep deprivation can be very subtle in children. They rarely complain of being tired—except when they are asked to clean their rooms. They generally make an effort to carry on with their normal activities. Children who are easily frustrated, quick to anger or tears, have a short attention span, or find it difficult to stick with a game or task, particularly in the late afternoon, may simply be tired. Once this situation is recognized and remedied, a child who was previously tolerable turns out to be terrific.

Children need adequate sleep to grow and develop optimally. Parents can ensure that this important need is satisfied by appropriately managing the child's bedtime.

6

~~~~~~

BEDTIME RITUALS

A pleasant bedtime ritual can be the key to avoiding nightly struggles about going to sleep. Bedtime battles occur for a variety of reasons. Children frequently procrastinate at bedtime because they do not want to miss out on the special events that they think take place after they are asleep. Other children fear the separation from loved ones that going to bed entails. Some children need a considerable amount of time to wind down from the activities of the day, to relax enough to sleep. They stall until they feel ready to go to bed.

A good bedtime ritual can meet the needs of children for security, love, and relaxation. This transition time can incorporate special traditions that make it a valued part of the day for all family members. A bedtime ritual can reflect the closeness and warmth that families strive for each day. In this way, bedtime becomes an integral part of the day rather than a time to be dreaded.

Although there is no set approach to designing bedtime rituals, the most effective share certain characteristics. A soothing and intimate routine promotes relaxation and a sense of security. Scary, violent, or rousing activities should be avoided. The routine should be consistent from night to night. The child is comforted by being able to predict what will happen at each step of the routine. Another consideration involves allowing the child to make choices. Selecting the book that is to be read, for instance, promotes mastery of the bedtime experience. The routine should involve both parents, if possible, and should be conducted at a leisurely pace. Most families set aside 20 minutes to a half an hour for this activity, but some children need as much as an hour of transition time. The time and attention help to reassure the child and dispel the fear that he is being excluded from a more exciting event taking place in another part of the house.

Developmental Factors

Another important factor that influences the bedtime routine is the child's developmental level. As the child grows and can participate more actively, the routine should change to accommodate new skills.

The bedtime ritual for an infant does not have to be elaborate. In many cases, these bedtime rituals develop naturally as the infant's behavior settles into a pattern. If this does not occur by six months, a routine should be instituted. This may involve a comforting physical activity, like rocking. Music, singing, and reading may also be important components. Following a short and calming transition time, the infant should be set down awake in the place where she is expected to sleep. More detailed information about infant bedtime rituals can be found in Key 10.

The ritual for a toddler is more complex, reflecting her more advanced developmental status. Toddlers can exercise some of their prized, newfound autonomy in an appropriate context by choosing between two books offered by the parents. Music continues to be an effective means of calming a child. Toddlers also love routines in which they can actively participate. Rituals in which parents and children take turns, for instance saying good night to objects in the room or to body parts, not only promote togetherness but stimulate the child's emerging language skills.

35

Another popular technique is to tell a story that recaps the events of the child's day. Being the central figure in the story really adds to a child's feeling of self-worth. In addition, as the child chimes in with her own recollections, the parents gain valuable insights into their child's world view.

Simple board games can be added to books and music for a preschooler's bedtime routine. Game playing provides an opportunity to explore significant concepts, such as fairness, taking turns, and adherence to rules. Games can also solidify cognitive advances in counting, number recognition, and color identification.

A preschooler's love of drama can be incorporated into the bedtime ritual. Family members can perform puppet shows or act out familiar stories. This is another opportunity to enhance a child's language skills, creativity, and imagination.

It is particularly critical with preschoolers to clarify how many books will be read or how many times a game will be played. Nothing disrupts the calm of a nice bedtime routine like a furious tantrum!

School-aged children should be encouraged to take more responsibility for their own bedtime routines. They may wish to have some private time before they go to sleep. They may choose to play quietly, listen to music, or read. School-aged children can put a twist on the tradition of the bedtime story by reading to their parents or younger siblings. Older children can tackle more complicated books by reading a chapter a night. This is an excellent family project that can promote a sense of closeness and shared purpose.

Transitional Objects

Just as the bedtime ritual serves as a bridge, so, too, can physical objects. A *transitional object* is a piece of the daytime world that the child can bring to bed to ease the process of nighttime separation.

Some children pick the object themselves, which might be a cuddly stuffed animal or a soft blanket. If a child has not selected an object, the parent can try to introduce one. A superb choice for an infant is an article of the parent's clothing, preferably unlaundered, that retains the parent's scent. Care must be taken that the garment does not pose a strangulation hazard. This type of transitional object allows the child to have a "piece" of the parent with her all night.

If a child becomes attached to a particular object, it is a good idea to line up a duplicate. Transitional objects may get lost, misplaced, or require washing.

A child may not form an attachment to one special object but may prefer to choose a different stuffed animal to take to bed with her each night.

Bedtime does not have to be the last battle of the day. With a suitable bedtime ritual, settling down for the night can be a positive experience. Families have risen to the challenge of the bedtime ritual by creating memorable and meaningful traditions. Several wonderful examples, which may serve as inspiration, are presented in detail in Key 7.

7

TOP BEDTIME RITUALS

Bedtime rituals are special—just like the families that establish them. The best are tailored to the needs, personality, and interests of the particular family. The bedtime ritual is not a static thing. As the developmental needs of the child change, the bedtime ritual, too, undergoes adaptation. The following are some ingenious ideas that can serve as wonderful endings to fun-filled days.

Let's Go to the Audio Tape

Family members can be tape recorded reading a favorite book. The child can even be involved in selecting some of the titles to be read. As the text is read, if the narrator indicates when to turn to the next page, a child with book in hand can actually "read" along. This is a nice way for relatives and friends who live at a distance to participate in an important family time. These tapes are invaluable to babysitters as well. The child can still have a bedtime story read by a parent while Mom and Dad are enjoying a night out. A variation on this theme is a tape of soothing music selected or sung by a special friend.

All About Eve

Children love to be the central figures in stories. Instead of reading books about other children, the events of the day can be used as the basis for a bedtime story. The traditional "Once upon a time" is a good opener, followed by "there was a terrific little girl named Eve" (or whatever the child's name happens to be). It is amazing how quickly children catch on to the fact that the story is really about them. They readily chime in with additions, corrections, or details about the day that the adults may scarcely have noticed. In this context, they volunteer information that is often impossible to obtain by direct questioning. The children's contributions, freely given, provide parents with unique insights into the children's world. These shared stories give parents an invaluable opportunity to understand their children's own values, thoughts, and feelings.

Still Crazy After All These Years

One of the reasons that children find bedtime so difficult is that they must deal with separation from the people they love the most. Telling children stories about when they were younger is a way that the family's continuity can be emphasized at this stressful time. Children adore hearing about the day they were born or their misadventures as toddlers. They may request the same tale over and over, just as they would a favorite book. Valuable security derives from the familiar and predictable conclusion. Looking at family photographs or a scrapbook evokes some of the same feelings. As they review the pictures, children can be reassured, in a very concrete way, of their essential place in the family structure. The celebrations, parties, and other special occasions depicted in the photographs are a tangible reminder of the warmth and love that families share.

Imagine

Some children just find it hard to wind down, physically, after an active day. Imagery may be helpful in relaxing a very energetic child sufficiently to fall asleep. A child who is visually oriented can be encouraged to picture a scene he finds relaxing. This might be floating on a cloud, lying on a warm beach, gliding in a canoe, or gently holding a soft, sleepy animal. Some children are immediately able to picture the scene in its entirety; others may need guidance from an adult in filling in the details of how things look, smell, and feel. As they concentrate on elaborating this imaginary world, the events and problems of the day become less important and relaxation can take place. An alternative technique has the child concentrate on quieting various parts of the body, starting with the toes and working all the way up to the head. A variation that is quite effective with a younger child is to have him say good night to the objects in his room. A chorus of "good nights" sets up a gentle rhythm that can lull a child to sleep. Listening to music may also help children relax. Music can be used by itself or in conjunction with one of the other visualization techniques described.

All Together Now

Another reason that children resist bedtime is their concern that they will miss something really exciting while they're asleep. This concern is heightened when a young child is sent off to bed while other family members remain engaged in an activity. One way to address this problem is to make the process of going to bed the focal point for the entire family. Turn off the television, set down the newspaper, and suspend work on the model allosaurus. Have all the family members march off together for changing into pajamas and brushing teeth. The child can then really concentrate on the task of getting ready for bed without being distracted or enticed by the sounds of activities taking place without him.

As Time Goes By

Bedtime difficulties are compounded by the child's poorly developed sense of time. To a child, bedtime can seem like a rotten or, at best, entirely arbitrary parental idea. Even a parent who tries to soften the blow of bedtime by giving a warning about how much playtime is left may be frustrated by the child's lack of understanding of the concept of "10 minutes." One way to make the amount of remaining playtime more concrete is by using a kitchen timer. The parent can set the timer for an interval with the understanding that playtime is over when the bell rings. This eliminates the need for repeated parental warnings and nagging. Children try to wheedle an extension from a parent, but they understand the futility of pleading with the timer and tend to respond more promptly. At this point, the timer can be reset and the child challenged to get ready for bed before the bell rings a second time.

Beethoven's Fifth

Many children dislike that final moment when the parents say good night and leave the room. One way to make leave-taking a bit more palatable is to offer to come back and check on the child in five minutes. At first, the child may fight sleep to make sure that the parents keep their promise. Sometimes there will be a chorus of "Is it five minutes yet?" or the child will make a personal appearance, reprimanding the parents for failing to check on him. If the parents consistently return after five minutes, the child is reassured and is able to fall asleep easily. The parents then find a sleeping child at the five-minute check.

All You Need Is Love

An ideal bedtime ritual sends the child to sleep on a positive note. One way this can be accomplished is by having the parents tell the child something they really love about him each night right before bedtime. This is a head start toward sweet dreams.

8

~~~~~~

THE BEDROOM ENVIRONMENT

T he bedroom should be a child's sanctuary. It is a place for his prized possessions, secret games, and special dreams. It should be a place of comfort, security, and safety. Sometimes the sign on the door says "Keep out" and other times parents are begged to stay for the night. This chapter explores some of the considerations in setting up a child's bedroom.

The Crib

The crib is usually the centerpiece of the baby's room. The most important factor, particularly if the crib is an old one, is whether it conforms to current safety standards. Crib slats should not be more than 2⅜ inches apart so that the baby cannot slip through the bars and strangle. If the crib is painted, the paint should be lead free to avoid lead poisoning in the infant.

An ideal crib has a mattress that can be lowered as the baby grows. Side rails that can be lowered on both sides provide maximum flexibility. The side rails should move quietly so that the baby is not awakened when they are raised or lowered. The side-rail tops should be covered with a plastic teething strip to prevent the infant from gnawing on the wooden rail itself.

The mattress should be designed for the specific crib model. The mattress should fit snugly in the crib, without spaces between it and the side rails where a baby could become wedged.

Mattresses are made of either coiled innersprings or foam rubber. Innerspring mattresses are generally more expensive and last longer. The price is determined by the number of coils and how they are constructed. Foam mattresses should be turned head to foot and back to front on a monthly basis to provide optimal support.

Firmness is an important consideration in selecting a mattress. Place a hand squarely on the mattress: this gives an idea of the support it can be expected to provide.

The mattress cover should be strong, easily cleaned, waterproof, and flame-retardant.

After all this attention to the crib, many new parents discover that their baby initially refuses to sleep there. Some babies find it hard to adjust to such a large open space after being cramped up in the uterus for nine months. A bassinet, cradle, or sufficiently padded dresser drawer are all suitable interim sleeping places. Nests or hammocks can be purchased and placed in the crib to make it a little more cozy. As the baby begins to grow, the mattress should be lowered successively so that the side rails reach at least the level of the child's shoulders when he's in a standing position.

Care should be taken with objects that are left in the crib. Bumper pads should be securely tied to the side rails. They should be removed once the child is able to stand because they can be bunched up and used as a step stool to climb out of the crib. Parents should be alert to other toys that can be used in the same way and remove them before bedtime. Small toys and rattles are hazards because they can become wedged in the baby's mouth. As the child begins to sit, parents should remove any toys hanging from bars across the crib because of the danger of strangulation.

Strings of any kind represent a strangulation threat. Parents should be careful about the length of the strings on the baby's clothing. A pacifier should *never* be placed on a string around the child's neck. Cribs should not be positioned next to windows where children might obtain access to the cords from window blinds.

The next level of development is heralded by the child's ability to climb out of the crib. Some children master this feat at quite an early age (a year or so); others are content to stay in the crib past age three.

For parents who cannot imagine placing a one year old in a bed, a crib net is a useful item. The net attaches to the rails, headboard, and footboard and zips closed at the top. Climbing out is effectively curtailed, and children adjust to this very well. (See the last part of this book for purchasing information.)

The Bed

The grown-up experience of sleeping in a real bed appeals to most children. The transition can be smoothed if they accompany their parents to the furniture store and contribute to the final decision. On occasion, the decision to move a child to a bed is prompted by a new baby's need for the crib. In this case, it is advisable to make the move to the bed at least two months in advance of the newborn's arrival. Otherwise, the child resents being stripped of his possession by the tiny invader, and the transition is more difficult.

Another tactic is to allow the child to sleep on the mattress on the floor until he gets used to it, and then set up the bed. Alternatively, the bed can be set up with one side against the wall and the crib mattress against the other side to cushion a fall. If it is possible to keep both the crib and bed set up simultaneously, the child can choose to make the move at his own pace.

Care at Night

A room may be made more hospitable by a night-light. If the child wants one, it is a good idea to let him select it. Make sure that the light it provides is sufficient to check a sleeping child. Other possibilities include using a hall or closet light or an overhead light on a dimmer switch.

Nighttime checks are best when they reassure the parent and do not disturb the baby. Make sure that the door to the room opens noiselessly, or leave it slightly ajar. Toys should be put away so that the parent does not trip over them. If the child's room is dark, the parent should keep a flashlight at the bedside to be used for nighttime checks. If the baby's diaper is to be changed at night, dressing him in a sleep sack that opens at the bottom makes the process easier. It is important that the parent's hands be warm: cold hands can startle a baby and wake him up.

Intercoms have positive and negative aspects. Babies normally make noises at night when they shift between sleep states. There are also times when they are up but are able to settle themselves back down without help. Parents who use intercoms should make sure that the baby really needs them before they intervene, and they should resist the temptation to respond to every squeak and whimper.

Sharing a Room

Children's views on sharing a room change with age. Young children like to have company at night; older children crave privacy. The presence of an older sibling may assuage a toddler's night fears. An older sibling may be more effective than a parent in curbing a young child's sleep disturbances. A single, firm "I'm sleeping. Don't bother me," from a revered older sibling can be immensely powerful. Sometimes the siblings must be separated because one is disturbing the other's sleep. In this case, the child can be promised that he will get his roommate back once his sleep behavior improves. This can work as a strong motivating force.

The bedroom should be a place of positive associations. It should not be the site of punishment or time-out. Sending the child to bed as a punishment should also be avoided. Attention to the bedroom environment ensures that it is a place of sweet dreams.

9

IN PRAISE OF NAPS

N aps are a wonderful invention. They provide both children and adults with an opportunity to refuel and face the rest of the day with energy and bonhomie.

The Infant Nap

Infants between six months and a year generally spend three hours a day napping. The time is usually organized into a one-hour morning nap and a two-hour afternoon nap.

The classic advice offered to parents of infants is to "nap when the baby naps." Parents are often in conflict about whether actually to follow this dictum. First-time parents, especially those who worked outside the home before the baby was born, fantasize about the new skills they will acquire during the vast stretches of time the baby is supposed to spend asleep. They collect exotic cookbooks, buy oil paints, and consider sitting down and writing the Great American Novel. When the baby is finally born, they realize that free moments are a rare commodity. When such moments arise, many competing interests vie for this precious time. Some of the more fanciful options are likely to be replaced by practical considerations, such as taking a shower or getting dressed. Considering how exhausting parenting is, even these mundane actions are great accomplishments.

There is one parental undertaking that should take precedence over all others. The single most important task in the first few months of life is the establishment of a

47

nurturing relationship with the infant. The interpersonal foundation laid down in infancy has lifelong implications. Parents must be well rested to meet the challenges of caring. It is good advice to nap when the baby naps.

The Toddler Nap

Toddlers usually nap for an hour or two each day, but the range is anywhere from 20 minutes to several hours. The nap usually takes place after lunch. Active toddlers may have difficulty settling down for a nap. All the techniques that are applicable to the bedtime routine can be employed at naptime, too. The consistency between the two routines may actually make the process easier, as the child comes to associate certain maneuvers with going to sleep. For some children, only a condensed version of the bedtime ritual is necessary at naptime.

Parents can make naps more attractive to toddlers. One technique is not to call them naps at all. The child may have negative associations with the word *nap* and therefore balk at resting. A less emotionally charged word may be better accepted. A child may protest at being placed in her crib, but she might view sleeping in a sleeping bag, lounge chair, tent, or nest made out of a large box filled with pillows as an adventure. Some children sleep particularly well out of doors. If the parents lie down, too, and the house is quiet, the child is more likely to sleep.

The Preschool Nap

Children stop taking a nap between three and five years of age. During the adjustment period, which can last three weeks, the child may be cranky and prone to temper tantrums in the late afternoon. An earlier dinner and bedtime may be helpful.

Preschoolers may not nap, but they do need some quiet time to refuel. An option is the video nap. Watching a nonviolent, not too stimulating video tape can provide just the respite the child needs. Sometimes the child actually falls asleep. Even if she does not, being occupied quietly for a half an hour is restorative.

The child is more likely to be cooperative with this scheme if she is not tempted by activities going on elsewhere in the house. This is a good time for the parent to sit down alongside the child and read a magazine or do some paperwork. Listening to music or playing with specially designated quiet-time toys are other ways to get a child to rest.

The Too Late Nap
The timing of naps is important. Sometimes it takes a baby a long time to settle down for a much needed nap, and she is still sound asleep at 5 P.M. A three year old may fall asleep in the late afternoon after a strenuous day at nursery school. Late naps on a regular basis, however, wreak havoc with bedtime. For most children, four to five hours must elapse between the end of the nap and bedtime. If the naps extends until 5:00 P.M., for instance, the child cannot realistically be expected to go to bed much before nine o'clock.

Naptimes can be moved up, but the changes must be made gradually. The best way to accomplish this is to set the child down for the nap 15 minutes earlier each day until the desired time is reached.

The Too Long Nap
Attention should be paid to the duration of the nap as well. The more the child sleeps during the day, the less she can be expected to sleep at night. If excessive daytime sleep interferes with the child's ability to sleep at night, she should be awakened after a suitable interval.

Waking a child from a nap can be tricky. This is one time when the parents' advances are most unwelcome. An indirect approach, in which the child rouses herself after mild parental stimulation, is usually best. Parents can accomplish this by opening the door to the child's room so she can hear household sounds, such as music playing or the water running in the kitchen. Some parents find it useful to putter around in the child's room. The child may be grouchy or disoriented for a few minutes after waking up from a nap. She may need some time to adjust before she can resume full activity. A snack can also help smooth this transition time.

Naps on the Go

Children tend to fall asleep in the car. If carpooling or errand time coincides with the time of the child's nap, this is perfect. If a late afternoon car nap interferes with bedtime, then some scheduling changes are necessary.

Napping when visiting or traveling poses special problems. Some children find it difficult to adjust to sleeping in a new environment. If the parent can arrange for parallels with home, the transition is easier. It is important to pack the treasured blanket or toy that the child is used to having in bed with her. If a child has a favorite audio tape for bedtime, this should be brought along, too. A night-light can make an unfamiliar room less threatening.

In the excitement of traveling, a family is often tempted to forego the child's nap. A midday break from the pace of sightseeing is probably a good idea for all family members. This is a fine time to unwind, study the map, or write postcards. A rest leaves everyone with more energy for the remainder of the afternoon and evening. In some areas, taking a break in the middle of the day is also a way of avoiding the hottest weather and the biggest crowds.

Getting a Child to Nap

It is not possible to force a child to nap any more than it is possible to force her to sleep at night. There are times when parents especially want the child to nap in anticipation of a special late night event, like the fireworks on the Fourth of July. These are just the times when the child resists. It is reasonable to spend an hour trying to induce a child to rest. If she has not fallen asleep after this interval, the issue should not be pursued further. It is unlikely at this point that the child will fall asleep, and the parent will just end up feeling angry and frustrated. If the child was at least quiet during this period, she might have gotten sufficient rest to tide her over for the festivities. If she falls asleep during the fireworks, there's always next year.

Naps provide a much-needed respite from the stresses of the day. Parents and children should enjoy them while they can.

10

~~~~~~

SLEEPING THROUGH THE NIGHT

P arents look forward to the time when their newborn infant sleeps through the night. Once the baby is able to sleep for several hours at a stretch, parents can start to make up for their own sleep deficits.

Sleep is not a homogeneous, unresponsive state that lasts eight hours a night. It is a much more dynamic state, comprised of alternating periods of quiet and active sleep. Brief periods of arousal also normally occur after some of the active sleeptimes. (More on the science of sleep can be found in Key 15.)

A baby is said to sleep through the night if he can sleep five to six hours at a stretch. Although this amount of sleep might not seem ideal from a family's point of view, this is the scientific definition used in medical studies. Seventy percent of three month olds, 83 percent of six month olds, and 90 percent of one year olds are able to sleep through the night.

The ability to string several sleep cycles together for a sleep period of five to six hours depends, in part, on the maturity of the brain and nervous system. The child who sleeps through the night has learned to put himself back to sleep after the normal brief arousal periods. There is no fundamental change in the structure of sleep. The periods of quiet and active sleep continue as before. The child has just learned to handle the normal night wakings without parental involvement.

This understanding has been confirmed by research studies in which video cameras were placed in infants' rooms to record their nighttime behavior. In one study of nine month olds, 84 percent were up one or more times during the night for a total of nine minutes. Because they went back to sleep on their own, however, their parents considered them to be sleeping through the night.

Feeding Practices

A baby who gets up to feed at 2 A.M. does not sleep through the night. By the time a baby reaches 12 pounds, he should be able to take a substantial enough late night feeding to hold him until the early morning. Some babies continue to wake up at 2 A.M. to feed long after the night feeding has ceased to be a nutritional necessity. For these babies, it has become a habit. Night feedings can be eliminated in a nontraumatic way that is described in Key 17. It is a good idea to check that the baby's growth is adequate before starting on such a program.

Exhausted parents whose baby is not yet sleeping through the night will try almost anything to remedy the situation. One piece of advice they often hear is to add cereal to the baby's last feeding of the day. The theory is that this heavier meal placates the baby until morning. There is no scientific proof that giving babies cereal helps them sleep longer. There is evidence, however, that the early introduction of solid food provokes allergies in susceptible children. It is a good idea to check with the baby's pediatrician before starting solid foods.

Although the capacity to sleep through the night is primarily neurologically determined, parents can take some measures.

53

Bedtime Routine

Most families fall into a pattern of activity at bedtime and then use this as the basis for the baby's bedtime routine. Some babies don't seem to have a set pattern at all. This may be temperamentally determined (see Key 11) or the product of a chaotic or stressful family life. If by six months no discernible pattern has emerged, parents can help by taking the initiative and providing structure.

A bedtime routine for an infant need not be elaborate. A warm, soothing bath is an excellent starting point. Motion and physical closeness are also calming. This may take the form of carrying the infant in a front pack, rocking in a rocking chair, or snuggling in an armchair with the infant against the parent's chest. The baby can be pushed in a carriage or placed in a windup swing. Springs can even be added to the baby's crib to make it bouncy. Some babies are comforted by having their arms crossed over their chests and held there with gentle pressure. Others like to be wrapped up snugly in a blanket. Another favored position is nestled in a corner of the crib against the bumper pads. It is currently recommended that healthy babies sleep on their backs or on their sides.

Sound is also an important element of an infant's bedtime routine. It is never too early to start reading to a baby (see the last part of this book for suggestions). In addition to producing pleasant sounds, the reader provides early language models. Singing or playing a musical instrument or an audio tape are other options. Various monotonous tones perform the double duty of lulling the baby to sleep while drowning out distracting household noises. These include the sounds made by appliances, such as hair dryers, fans, and vaporizers. These sounds can be tape recorded and played in the baby's room at bedtime. Another important bedtime ally is the dishwasher. The gurgling sounds made by the cascading water are thought to be similar to what the baby heard in the uterus. A tape of these sounds at bedtime may be comforting.

Schedules

A consistent schedule facilitates settling. If the baby always has a bath, followed by a story, a good-night kiss, and sleep, these individual elements join to form a seamless whole. The baby comes to expect this pattern and accepts the flow from one element to the next. This association grows even stronger as the baby develops the capacity to anticipate events, and thus the transition is smoother. By the time the baby becomes a toddler, the routine is so ingrained that not a single deviation is tolerated.

An erratic schedule, in contrast, means starting from the ground up each night. There are no continuities for the baby to discover and anticipate. The baby ends up being much more dependent and passive at night, and the parents end up doing much more of the work.

Sleeping Together

At the time that the parents expect the baby to sleep through the night, a decision should be made about the family bed. Until this time, when the baby is feeding frequently at night, it is often much easier to have the baby in the parents' room. If this arrangement continues after the baby has stopped feeding at night, it becomes part of his associations with sleep. The longer it continues, the more difficult it is to disrupt this established custom.

If parents do not want the infant to sleep in their room, the cessation of night feeding represents a natural break point. This is an ideal time to move the baby to his room and set up new associations with sleep. Whatever the family's preference, this is a decision that is best made early. A young child who is used to sleeping alone may have difficulty adjusting to the family bed. There are also painful adaptations in store for a child who is used to having company at night and then suddenly finds himself sleeping alone.

Intercoms

Intercoms have good and bad points. For some parents, knowing that they can hear a child in distress allows them to relax and go to sleep. Other parents toss and turn as they listen to the nightly concert provided by their offspring. Babies make a variety of sounds at night. They move around in the crib. They may cry or whimper, especially during the brief arousal periods. Most often they go back to sleep if left to their own devices. If parents respond to every sound heard over the intercom, they interfere with this natural process and deprive the infant of the experience of learning how to handle these arousal periods. Parents should allow their infants several minutes to settle themselves. If hearing all the sounds makes it impossible to resist going to the baby's room, another option is to turn off the intercom for a time.

Sleep Associations

The way a baby handles nighttime arousals is influenced by his sleep onset associations. *Sleep onset associations* are the conditions under which an individual initially falls asleep. For a baby to sleep through the night, he must be able to re-create his own sleep onset associations after a night waking. A baby who is used to falling asleep in his crib can settle himself down, just as he did originally, after a night waking. Another baby who is used to falling asleep in someone's arms does not know what to do when he finds himself awake later in his crib. His sleep onset associations are not intact. He cries until someone comes in to restore them by rocking him back to sleep. Parents must think about the baby's sleep onset associations as they set up the initial falling-to-sleep mode. Many difficulties can be avoided if the baby is put to sleep in the same place he will find himself later, should he wake at night. (For more detailed information on sleep onset associations, see Key 16.)

Sleeping through the night is a milestone for infants and a blessing for their parents. An understanding of its scientific and environmental underpinnings can at least make the wait more bearable.

11

~~~~~~

TEMPERAMENT AND SLEEP

Patty was a delightful baby. She always seemed to be in a good mood. She responded positively to new people and new experiences. Caretaking was easy because of the regularity of her schedule. She awoke at amazingly precise three-hour intervals for her feedings. Even her bowel movements occurred at the same time every day.

John was a very different infant. He was cranky and fussy most of the time. His daily schedule was totally unpredictable. One afternoon he would take a three-hour nap, and the next day he would sleep for only 30 minutes. His food intake was erratic as well. He would take as little as $1\frac{1}{2}$ ounces or as much as 6 ounces at a single feeding.

It was not very hard to discern John's strong opinions. He hated bananas and loved squash. When he was fed bananas, John would spit the mouthful of food across the room. During a meal that included squash, he would squeal and laugh and grin from ear to ear.

John was always an active baby. Mrs. Frances had to go to him numerous times each night because he kept kicking off the covers. Mrs. Frances recalled that he had been quite active in the uterus, too. He kicked so much that she and her husband used to refer to him as Pelé, the soccer player.

Babies are born with a constellation of personality and behavioral characteristics that have been labeled "temperament." Babies with different temperaments have different behavior patterns and thrive under different caretaking conditions. The more parents know about their baby's temperament, the better they can understand their baby, derive appropriate expectations, and provide individualized, responsive care.

The Temperamental Traits

There are nine traits that, taken together, constitute a child's temperament: activity level, distractability, intensity of reaction, regularity, persistence, sensory threshold, approach and withdrawal, adaptability, and mood.

The Easy Baby

Most children are like Patty, a temperamentally easy baby. It is a pleasure to take care of a baby who is usually happy, accepting of new experiences, adaptable, and mild in intensity. That she established a regular pattern in all her bodily functions is also a distinct advantage.

An easy baby establishes a regular daily pattern of sleep and wakefulness. Naptimes are predictable, and the total duration of sleep is often constant from day to day. Parents can read an easy baby's clear behavioral signals and know when she is tired. She does not need help to fall asleep. She can be set down awake in the crib and soothes herself until she drifts off to sleep. An easy baby spends long periods of time in deep sleep. She does not even cry out during the brief arousals between sleep states.

The Difficult Baby

A baby like John is a challenge to any parent. On the basis of his traits of negative mood, irregularity of schedule, intensity of reaction, initial withdrawal, and high activity level, he would be characterized as a child with a difficult temperament.

A difficult baby exhibits no discernible pattern in sleep-wake activity. He requires help from the environment to establish a pattern, but it is harder to read his cues. Since he has trouble adapting, the transition from wakefulness to sleep can be problematic. It takes a difficult baby more time to fall asleep. Parents find that providing extrinsic soothing can assist him in making the transition. Swaddling the baby, placing him in a swing, walking with him in a front pack, or going for a car ride may be helpful. He comes to depend on these aids, and thus it takes him longer to learn how to comfort himself at bedtime.

A difficult baby often has a shorter total daily sleep duration than an easy baby. He sleeps two hours less during the night and one hour less during the day. Given this, and the unpredictability of his schedule, it is critical that parents of a difficult baby sleep when he sleeps. A difficult baby spends more time in active sleep. He is likely to have more periods of wakefulness and crying because active sleep is more vulnerable to environmental disturbances.

The Slow to Warm up Child

The third temperament type is the slow to warm up child. These children typically have a low activity level and a tendency to withdraw on initial exposure to a new situation. They are slow to adapt and low in intensity.

It is important to realize that all the temperament types—difficult, easy, and slow to warm up—are normal. There is no one type that is intrinsically better or worse than the others. Temperament is inborn, not a reflection of parental competence. Wonderful parents can have difficult or easy children.

Parents do not necessarily have the same temperament as their children. Siblings, too, may be temperamen-

tally different from one another. Some kinds of temperament pairings are particularly challenging. Easy parents
must develop new skills to deal with difficult children.
Parents who feel comfortable with difficult temperaments
may consider an easy child shockingly lacking in verve.

Temperament is a key determinant of behavior during
both the waking and sleeping states. Parents who understand their child's temperamental characteristics find it
easier to understand their child's behavior. They are able to
respond to the particular needs of their child. They are able
to anticipate that an easy baby will make a smoother
transition from the two-nap stage to the one-nap stage than
a child with a difficult temperament. They are able to
provide the additional support that a slow to warm up child
needs to adjust to a new bed. There are numerous other
ways in which a knowledge of temperament allows parents
to modify the environment, avert conflicts, and assist the
child in his or her development.

A knowledge of temperament can also decrease a
parent's stress and guilt. It is reassuring to know a child's
difficult temperament is intrinsic, not the product of
parental ineptitude. It is comforting to learn that anyone
would find it a challenge to be the child's parent. It is not
easy to live with a child who does not settle down into a
pattern and who sleeps restlessly. Knowing the reason for
this behavior, however, can at least provide some solace.

12

COSLEEPING

The question of whether children should sleep in the parents' bed is eventually faced by every family. This is not an issue with obvious right and wrong answers. This is an area in which a family makes a choice after considering their values and philosophy of child rearing. What is optimal for one family is not necessarily optimal for another. The most important thing, whatever the final decision, is that the family is comfortable with their choice. In this chapter, the advantages and disadvantages of cosleeping are explored. This will help families make informed decisions on this controversial topic.

Cosleeping means that children and their parents share a common sleeping space. Cosleeping can take a number of different forms. It does not necessarily mean that all family members sleep in the same bed. This would be a hardship with a small bed or a child who is an active sleeper. Other arrangements include moving the child's crib into the parents' room and placing it next to the parents' bed. An older child can sleep on a mattress or sleeping bag.

A more restrictive kind of cosleeping allows the children in the parents' bed only under special circumstances. Proponents of this view believe that it represents a good compromise between the children's need for closeness and the parents' need for privacy. The children might be welcome in their parents' bed, for instance, in the early mornings or on weekends. Other families make exceptions only on sporadic occasions, such as when a child is ill or has had a nightmare and requires comforting. Parents must be very clear about when the children are allowed in their bed if they want to avoid constant battles over these limits.

The Advantages of Cosleeping

Advocates of cosleeping believe that parents should be available to the child both day and night. Sleeping together is only one facet of this availability. They claim that cosleeping makes a child happier, more secure, and less dependent. They feel that sleeping together conveys a message of caring to the child.

Cosleeping does make it easier to meet a child's nighttime needs. If the child requires feeding or comforting during the night, he is close by. He can be tended to quickly before he becomes completely upset. The child experiences closeness with the parents by being able to touch or see them throughout the night. Bedtime is no longer a threat because it is no longer a time of separation. There are reports that children have fewer night wakings and nightmares when they sleep with their parents. There are even claims that children and parents who sleep together have synchronized sleep cycles. Cosleeping has a long historical tradition and is practiced by many cultures worldwide.

The Advantages of Separate Sleep Spaces

Advocates for separate sleep spaces believe that the ability to sleep alone is a learned skill. If children do not have an opportunity to sleep by themselves, they do not have a chance to master this ability. Proponents of this point of view believe that a child who sleeps with his parents is more likely to be dependent, anxious, and socially immature. They also fear that the child whose parents are on 24-hour call will turn out to be spoiled.

Parents who do not favor cosleeping also cite their own needs. They desire some time apart from their children to refuel for the following day. For many parents, private space that is not accessible to the children is central to the refueling process. Parents are also concerned about the impact of cosleeping on their own sexual spontaneity.

Making a Decision

Decisions about sleeping arrangements should ideally be made during infancy. It is confusing to a child to start with one arrangement and then suddenly switch to another. Cosleeping can involve a long-term commitment. Advocates of cosleeping advise waiting for the child to indicate that he is ready to leave the family bed. This generally occurs within the second or third year of life.

It is important that the decision be one that both parents support. If one parent is unhappy about the sleeping arrangements, this tension is communicated to the child.

Parents also need to be aware of the motivations behind their decision making. Sometimes, parents allow a child who wakes frequently during the night to sleep with them out of sheer desperation. They are tired of making multiple trips to the child's room at night, and sleeping together cuts down on mileage. The child usually sleeps well in the parents' bed, but the parents often feel intruded upon and resentful. In this situation, it might be preferable to work on the child's night-waking behavior rather than substitute one problem for another.

A parent whose spouse travels frequently or works the night shift may view cosleeping as an attractive alternative to loneliness. It is important to remember that the rationale for cosleeping is the fulfillment of the child's needs. Cosleeping was never intended to foist a burdensome role of spouse substitute on the child.

Healthy and well-adjusted children can be raised with either sleeping arrangement. Children can learn to accept limits on parental accessibility at night, provided that their needs are met during the day. Allowing a child in the parents' bed is not a panacea if it is done for the wrong reasons. Parents must weigh the togetherness factor and the privacy factor and arrive at a decision. If parents believe in the decision they have made, the children come to accept it.

Part Three

DEALING WITH SLEEP
PROBLEMS

13

SOLVING SLEEP PROBLEMS

Mrs. David had not enjoyed a full night's sleep in 912 consecutive nights. Her 2½-year-old daughter, Sharon, awoke crying several times each night. Mrs. David would then go to her and rock her back to sleep. Every night when Mrs. David tucked her daughter into bed, she recited a silent plea that she would not see Sharon until morning. But night after night, Sharon's behavior showed no indication of change.

Mrs. David, a first-grade teacher, exhausted and three months pregnant with her second child, bought a shelf load of books on how to get your child to sleep through the night. She crafted a plan. At three o'clock in the morning, however, with Sharon crying and her husband insisting that he needed his sleep, Mrs. David doubted that any of the suggested treatments really worked. In sheer desperation, she called the American Sleep Disorders Association and located a sleep disorders center not far from her home.

The Davids are in good company. Community surveys indicate that 20 to 30 percent of children under the age of five have sleep problems. Pediatricians report that concerns about sleep are the most common complaints they encounter in practice.

Barriers to Seeking Help

Unfortunately, many families do not get the help they need. Some parents think that they must accept a child's sleep problem just as they do any fixed aspect of the child's physique, such as the color of her eyes or the shape of her nose. These parents believe that tolerating sleepless nights is part of the job.

Parents sometimes fail to act on a sleep problem because they believe it is selfish to change the child's behavior just because they are fatigued. This "too nice" attitude is precisely what is responsible for the development of some sleep problems in the first place. Mrs. David was such a concerned, responsive, and loving mother that she never made Sharon responsible for her nighttime behavior. Mrs. David was always there to help Sharon settle back down after her night wakings. Sharon, as expected, showed no signs of giving up a good thing 2½ years later, and Mrs. David was at her wit's end.

It is not selfish for parents to want to sleep through the night. Parents cannot function in a high-quality way 24 hours a day. They cannot tend to a child's needs if they are exhausted, angry, or depressed. Sleep deprivation can lead to marital problems and child abuse. A child's sleep problems can also affect siblings and other members of the household. Even neighbors may be disturbed by the child's crying at night. Parents who come in for help show true consideration for the child by trying to fulfill their familial responsibilities.

Other parents don't seek help because they do not recognize the sequellae of poor sleep in the child, which include poor coordination, overactivity, irritability, short attention span, and impatience. With some children, the effects of inadequate sleep are more subtle. In these cases it is only in retrospect, after the sleep problem is resolved, that the family discovers how much better the child can actually function.

Some parents, like Mrs. David, are optimistic people and hope each night for a spontaneous cure. This is, of course, much easier than the work of changing a child's behavior patterns. Spontaneous cures rarely occur. This is because a child needs motivation to change her behavior. Sharon got her mother's attention, both day and night, on demand. There is no conceivable reason for her wanting to alter this arrangement. An added complication is that the longer the situation continues, the more resistant it is to change.

Formal studies corroborate this observation. In one study, only 10 percent of sleep problems resolved without intervention. In the instances when this occurred, the average time to resolution was 17 months. In contrast, families that sought professional help solved their problems in an average of 10 days.

Some parents do not know where to turn for assistance. In one survey, only 56 percent of parents consulted the child's pediatrician. Guidance came primarily from friends and family. Their ideas ranged from reassurance that the child would grow out of it to a suggestion that she be placed in an adult-sized bed. The most commonly heard piece of advice was to let the child cry it out. This is very hard for parents to do and rough on the child, as well. Most parents find that they cannot follow through with this approach and end up going in to the child after a lengthy crying period. What the child learns from this experience is that her parents will eventually relent if she cries long enough.

Resourceful parents, like Mrs. David, consult self-help books. She was able to map out what, in the daytime, seemed like a reasonable and infallible plan. At three o'clock in the morning, however, with the pressure of Sharon crying hysterically and her husband screaming about a very important breakfast meeting he had to attend, the new program was not very appealing. It just seemed easier at the time to go in to Sharon and rethink the problem in the morning.

So what does it take to put an end to a child's sleep problem?

The Role of the Parents

The key ingredient for change is strong motivation on the part of the parents. Both parents must be convinced that it is in everyone's interest to change the child's sleep habits.

Parents must understand that it takes a concerted effort to change a long-standing behavior. They will be providing the impetus for change. They must expect that the child will react to the new bedtime regimen by expressing her outrage and dismay. She will fuss and cry and test the parents' resolve to follow through with the new program. To survive this challenge, parents must hold fast to their conviction that change at this time is better for all concerned. The child's short-term distress will be more than compensated by interaction with happier and more energetic parents. Parents can be assured that the crying does not lead to emotional problems.

During this interval of nighttime upheaval, parents should pay special attention to the quality of the daytime interaction with the child. They should make a point of providing lots of positive and supportive attention. If the child is old enough, the plan should be discussed directly with her before it is implemented.

Parents should carefully select the time they will enact a new behavioral plan. Ideally, this should be a time free from other stresses. It should not be a time when, for instance, the family is moving, the parents have increased responsibilities at work, or the child is adjusting to a new day-care situation. Some families choose to implement a plan when they're on vacation—far from the thin walls of neighboring apartments. Initiating the plan on a Friday night is beneficial because some of the lost sleep can be made up during the weekend.

Parents need to be firm and consistent in their approach. They must also implement the plan with confidence. A child can sense parental ambivalence and will react by escalating her resistance. Once a child realizes that the parents are committed to the new arrangement, she will adjust more quickly.

Both parents must believe in and be comfortable with the details of their plan. Even if one parent is primarily responsible for implementation, the spouse's support is critical. The plan should be individually tailored to the family's unique circumstances. It should take into account how long the parents can allow the child to cry and the pace at which they think it is appropriate to move. Parents should make nightly notes about their nocturnal activities. (See Table 13.1) These notes help parents avoid programmatic pitfalls and serve as evidence of their progress.

Table 13.1
NIGHT-WAKING CHART

	Night 1	Night 2	Night 3
Episode 1			
Time began			
Child's behavior			
Time entered room			
Intervention			
Time of next visit			
Time of next visit			
Time of next visit			
Child returned to sleep			
Episode 2			
Time began			
Child's behavior			
Time entered room			
Intervention			
Time of next visit			
Time of next visit			
Time of next visit			
Child returned to sleep			
Episode 3			
Time began			
Child's behavior			
Time entered room			
Intervention			
Time of next visit			
Time of next visit			
Time of next visit			
Child returned to sleep			

Working with a Sleep Specialist

The crafting of a plan is one area in which a sleep specialist, working closely with the family, can make an important contribution. Following an expert's plan helps to deflect those middle-of-the-night doubts. The specialist supports the parents when they are discouraged and will

73

review their notes to ensure they are progressing in the most effective way.

There are some things that a specialist cannot do. She cannot make a house call and fix the family's problem. Behavior problems are not like broken appliances. Behavior problems emerge in the context of the family and must be solved by the family. Many sleep problems are more about limit setting than they are about sleep. Parents need to learn how to set limits for their children. Children need to learn to respond to parental limits. The lessons learned in the context of solving a sleep problem can be applied to many other aspects of parent-child interaction.

This same type of explanation accounts for why children are not admitted to the hospital for treatment of sleep problems. Sleep problems need to be solved at home. Sleep in the hospital is different from sleep at home. In the hospital the bed is different, the room is different, and the ambient sounds are different. Children's sleep associations must be grounded in their everyday experience.

Sedative medication is not usually prescribed except in the most dire circumstances. A child may sleep under the influence of medication, but this approach merely masks the symptom without addressing the underlying problem. It is not an acceptable long-term solution. Efforts are better directed at identifying and treating the source of the child's difficulties.

There are benefits to solving sleep problems that go beyond everyone being better rested. Parental confidence increases as a result of having dealt successfully with a challenging situation. The parents have had the experience of working as a harmonious team. They have followed a plan with courage and determination. Most important, they have learned that they have the strength to handle the challenges that parenthood brings.

14

COPING WITH SLEEP PROBLEMS

T he toll in sleep disorders is often greater on the family than it is on the child. The child has the luxury of being able to drop off to sleep in the middle of the day. Tired parents have errands, jobs, obligations, and schedules that do not lend themselves to spontaneous rest periods. Sleep deprivation has an emotional side in addition to the physical. It leaves parents feeling angry, resentful, and powerless. This chapter examines the coping strategies available to parents of a child with a sleep problem.

Reduce Expectations

It is not reasonable to expect that a sleep-deprived parent will be able to cook gourmet meals, keep the silverware polished, and be conversant with the plots of the latest bestsellers. Dust balls are likely to gather under the couch.

The priority for a parent's limited resources should be nurturing the child. Concerns about housework only create additional stress, which saps the parent's finite strength. Although an extra pair of hands can be hired to help with the chores, no one but the parent can fulfill the parent's special role with the child.

Sleep When the Baby Sleeps

This commonly offered advice can be hard to follow at first. Once the baby shuts her eyes, the parent is pulled in a million different directions. Preserving parental energy reserves should be a first priority. A tired parent is not functioning at top capacity and is probably not having much fun, either. Sleeping when there is an opportunity is especially important if the baby wakes frequently at night and the parent cannot depend on getting an unbroken night's sleep. Disruptions can be minimized by taking the telephone off the hook or turning on the answering machine. A compromise for the ultracompulsive parent is to settle down when the baby does and set an alarm clock or timer for 30 or 45 minutes. This will ideally allow the parent enough time for a personal project before the baby wakes. Sometimes, the parent sleeps through the alarm. This should not be seen as a failure but as an indication of how much the sleep was needed.

Share the Weekends

Parents cannot depend on making up their sleep deficits on the weekends. Infants must be fed, changed, and reassured that their loved ones have not disappeared overnight. Older children can amuse themselves for awhile with quiet games, books, television, or videos. Eventually, however, parents will be awakened by an ominous clattering from the kitchen, where the children are trying to prepare them breakfast in bed.

A share-the-weekend plan allows at least one parent to luxuriate in bed while the other serves as the parent on duty. The parent on duty has a nice opportunity to spend some one-on-one time with the child. The parent on duty and the child may develop their own special customs, such as taking a jog together or going out for breakfast at the local coffee shop.

The sleep-in parent may not actually sleep but take the time to catch up on correspondence or to have an uninterrupted telephone conversation. A night owl parent may choose to stay up late the night before and work while the house is quiet, knowing that there will be a few extra hours of sleep in the morning.

Find a Babysitter

When a parent rises frequently at night and does not get adequate amounts of deep sleep, sleep deprivation occurs. Sleep deprivation can be devastating. It can take the joy out of parenthood. It can lead to depression, weight loss, marital problems, and child abuse.

Sleep deprivation is different from staying up all night once in awhile to study for a test or to finish a project. Sleep deprivation occurs when the sleep loss is chronic. Because there is a cumulative loss of deep sleep, it cannot be remedied by a nap the following day or a single good night's sleep. The parent requires solid sleep opportunities to begin the recovery process.

An option is to find someone to look after the baby so the parent can make up some sleep time. Grandparents, neighbors, or students are ideal candidates. If finances are a problem, a cooperative arrangement with another parent can ultimately benefit both parties.

Imagery

Imagery can be used to provide a minivacation. The parent should sit in a comfortable place and mentally re-create the sensations associated with a relaxing circumstance. This might be sitting on a warm beach, swinging in a hammock, or floating in the water. Only 5 to 15 minutes spent this way can leave a person feeling rejuvenated.

Identify and Reach out to Community Resources

Being a parent is an enormous responsibility. There may be times when an exhausted parent is not up to the challenge. A sleep-deprived parent can feel angry, impatient, or resentful toward the infant. Sometimes, in this situation, a parent worries about lashing out at the infant. Talking to a trained professional can provide an outlet for these feelings that does not involve harming the infant. Parents Anonymous is one such help line. They can be reached at (800) 421-0353.

The child's pediatrician is also an important resource. Sleep problems can be solved. Parents do not have to endure year after year of sleepless nights waiting for a spontaneous cure. If the child's pediatrician does not regularly inquire about the child's sleep behavior, the parent should bring it up. If the problem is beyond the pediatrician's expertise, a consultation with a specialist should be arranged.

Expect the Unexpected

Sleep problems seem to emerge at the most inopportune times. A child takes a 5 P.M. nap and undoes his regular bedtime on the very night when a parent needs several uninterrupted hours to work on an urgent project. If a parent has an early morning meeting, he can almost predict that the child will get up many times the night before. A parent with writer's block and a paper due first thing in the morning is greeted at midnight by a toddler offering to help.

The best approach in these predicaments is to stay calm and avoid a battle. Rushing the child back to bed never works because he senses that he's being given short shrift and he responds by resisting sleep. These are special situations that call for making exceptions to the usual rules. Allow the child to stay up to help. A young child can be placed in an infant swing or playpen with a few quiet toys. An older child can be told that he can stay up provided that he does not interfere with the work. He can watch a video (with the sound off, if necessary) or actually assist with small jobs, such as stapling or carting crumpled papers to the garbage. Sometimes, the experience is so boring that the child falls asleep or returns to bed voluntarily.

Parents who are coping with sleep problems can help themselves by trimming extraneous responsibilities, being flexible, and calling in the reinforcements.

15

THE SCIENCE OF SLEEP

S leep is a much more complex and active state than most people realize. This chapter covers some aspects of sleep physiology that are important to understanding normal sleep and sleep problems.

Everyone experiences two different kinds of sleep at night. Although the sleeper is not aware of these different types of sleep, they can be easily distinguished on the basis of brain wave tracings.

REM Sleep

REM (rapid eye movement) sleep is named for the bursts of eye movements that characterize it. If one looks at the thin, closed eyelids of a sleeping newborn, the darting movements of the eyes during REM sleep can sometimes be observed underneath. Another term for REM sleep is "active sleep." Blood pressure and blood flow to the brain increase during REM sleep. Females have clitoral engorgement and males have penile erections. The heart and breathing rates become irregular. Muscle tone is decreased, and there is little body movement. Complex, coordinated movements are impossible during REM sleep because nerve impulses from the brain to the muscles are mostly blocked. The movements that occur are associated with breathing, hearing, and the eyes. There may be occasional twitches of the hands, legs, or face. When awakened from REM sleep, a person becomes alert quickly.

REM sleep is the time that dreaming occurs. Although a person may not remember a dream every morning, there are periods of REM every night. Most REM sleep is concentrated in the early morning hours.

At the end of a REM period, it is normal for a child to have a brief arousal. The child may move around, check his environment to make sure that everything is normal, make minor adjustments, such as pulling up the covers, and return rapidly to sleep. If the environment is not the same as it was when he went to sleep, the original conditions must be restored before he is able to go back to sleep. This is one of the most frequent causes of sleep problems in the young child. The problem can be avoided if the child learns to fall asleep under the same conditions that he will experience later during the night.

Non-REM Sleep

The other kind of sleep is *non-REM sleep*. Non-REM is also termed "quiet sleep." A period of non-REM sleep leaves a person feeling refreshed. During non-REM sleep, the heart and breathing rates are stable. The muscles are relaxed, and the person lies quietly, although he retains the ability to move. There are four stages of non-REM sleep, ranging from drowsiness (stage I) to deep sleep (stage IV). The various stages can be identified by their distinct brain wave patterns. The bulk of non-REM sleep occurs in the first several hours after falling asleep.

A common experience of non-REM sleep is the *hypnagogic startle*. This is a total body jerking movement that occurs as one is falling asleep, which may even be strong enough to cause a brief awakening. It occurs during the descent into deep sleep. Other phenomena associated with non-REM sleep include night terrors, sleeptalking, and sleepwalking.

81

It is difficult to wake someone who is in stage IV sleep. A child often falls asleep in the car on the way home from a late night excursion. Parents find that they are able to lift him out of the car seat, carry him upstairs, undress him, put on his pajamas, and tuck him into bed without his even stirring. This is characteristic stage IV sleep behavior.

A powerful stimulus, such as a scream or the ringing of a telephone, can rouse an adult from stage IV sleep. The person is sufficiently coordinated, physically, to answer the phone but mentally foggy and unable to formulate an emergency response for a period of time.

A child may have brief partial wakings at the end of non-REM sleep periods. These look quite different from those associated with REM sleep. The child may sit up, open his eyes and stare blankly, make chewing movements, cry out, or mumble unintelligibly. All these behaviors are normal.

Sleep Patterns

REM and non-REM sleep periods alternate throughout the night in cycles. A sleep cycle is defined as the time between two consecutive appearances of the same sleep state. Sleep cycles last about 50 minutes in the newborn and 90 minutes in the adolescent and the adult.

The relative proportion of REM and non-REM sleep changes over the course of the night. By about three months, the infant assumes the adult pattern. He enters sleep through non-REM and usually is in stage IV within 10 minutes. He spends about an hour in stage IV, followed by a brief arousal of a few minutes' duration. Then there may be a short, 5- to 10-minute, REM period. Another similar pattern of 40 to 50 minutes in non-REM, arousal, and 15 to 20 minutes of REM sleep follows. Over the next several hours, the child alternates between REM and stage

II non-REM sleep. There may be one more period of stage III or stage IV sleep in the early morning particularly in young children. Thus, most of the deep sleep occurs during the first several hours after bedtime. Dreaming occurs primarily in the early morning hours. It is normal to have frequent brief arousals throughout the night.

Developmental Aspects of Sleep

There is also a developmental aspect to sleep. Premature infants, full-term infants, and older children all have different patterns of sleep.

Sleep patterns can actually be recognized in the fetus. REM sleep can be identified at six or seven months' gestation. Non-REM can first be seen at seven or eight months' gestation. Even at term, non-REM sleep is not fully developed. The four distinct stages of non-REM sleep are generally not seen until six months of age.

The amount of time spent in REM sleep decreases with age. Premature infants spend 80 percent of their sleep time in REM. For full-term newborns, REM represents 50 percent of sleep time. This percentage decreases to 33 percent for three year olds and to 25 percent in the older child, adolescent, and adult. It is believed that there is a preponderance of REM sleep early in life because it is important to the ongoing development of the brain. Non-REM sleep requires a higher degree of brain maturation, which is the reason it is not seen until a later age.

Sleeping like a baby is a complex phenomenon. Knowledge of the characteristics of sleep makes it possible to appreciate normal sleep and to understand the origins of various sleep disorders.

16

~~~~~~

SLEEP ONSET
ASSOCIATIONS

- *Sherry, aged 8 months, always fell asleep with a pacifier in her mouth.*
- *Danny, aged 15 months, could not fall asleep unless he was pushed in his stroller.*
- *Lauren, aged three years, insisted that one of her parents lie down in the bed with her until she fell asleep.*

During the course of every night, Sherry, Danny, and Lauren woke up several times. They cried until their parents came in to attend to them. The parents eventually discovered that they could get their children back to sleep if they repeated the going-to-bed ritual. Sometimes they had to put the children to bed three or four times in a single night.

One night, Sherry's mother felt she could not cope with the situation any longer. She decided to let Sherry cry it out. After listening to her daughter cry for 90 minutes, however, she relented and brought her another pacifier.

Crying it out didn't work for Danny's family, either. The night Danny was left to cry he got so upset that he vomited all over the crib.

Lauren's parents decided it would just be easier if they took turns sleeping with her. They were concerned that their daughter's screams would annoy the elderly couple who lived in the apartment next door.

During the daytime, the children were fine. They were bright and happy. Their parents, however, were exhausted, resentful, and utterly frustrated. Danny's mother felt that she was at her wit's end. Lauren's father described his daughter as Dr. Jekyll and Mr. Hyde.

S herry's, Danny's, and Lauren's sleep difficulties were related to their sleep onset associations. Sleep onset associations are the conditions that must be in place for a person to fall asleep.

What Are Sleep Onset Associations?

Everyone has sleep onset associations. Adults may get into the habit of reading, listening to music, or watching the 11 o'clock news before going to bed. People become used to particular physical factors, such as the firmness of their mattresses, the softness of their pillows, and the sounds of the traffic outside their bedroom windows.

Sleep onset associations may be taken for granted until a person tries to fall asleep in a new place. In a hotel room, for instance, the bed feels different and the street sounds are unfamiliar. Without their usual sleep onset associations, people find it more difficult to relax and fall asleep.

Sleep onset associations are also important during the course of the night. People normally awaken periodically during the night and check out the environment. Is the blanket still tucked in? Is the pillow scrunched up the right way? Is the room sufficiently dark? If the situation remains as it was when the person initially went to sleep, he is able promptly to return to sleep. If it is not, the original sleep onset associations must be restored before sleep can be resumed.

85

When Sherry awakened at night, the pacifier was no longer in her mouth. Danny found himself in the crib, not in the stroller. Lauren discovered that there was no parent sleeping beside her. None of the children were in the same circumstances that they had been in when they originally went to sleep. None of them could restore their sleep onset associations on their own. Their only recourse was to cry and have their parents come in and make things right.

Changing Sleep Onset Associations

There is an alternative to the prospect of year after year of sleepless nights. It involves gradually and gently reshaping the child's sleep onset associations. Once the child is able to reestablish his own sleep onset associations, he can be self-sufficient at night. This process always works, provided the parents are highly motivated and capable of implementing a plan firmly and consistently.

The first step is to identify the child's sleep onset associations. For Sherry, it was sucking on a pacifier. For Danny, it was the motion of the stroller. Lauren's association was snuggling with a parent.

The next step is to imagine a bedtime without the inappropriate sleep onset association. In Sherry's situation, this would mean going to bed without a pacifier. Danny would have to be placed right in the crib. Lauren would be expected to sleep in her bed by herself.

Parents can choose how quickly or slowly they wish to move to the new situation. A dramatic and abrupt change results in an intense reaction. It may take longer to reach a goal through gradual change, but the process may be easier to tolerate.

Parents need to understand that the child will actively resist these alterations in his routine. There is no way that a change of this magnitude can be achieved without some short-term unhappiness on the child's part. The child has no way of knowing that the new system will, ultimately, be beneficial to him. Sleeping through the night will mean he has more energy for daytime play. Better rested parents will be livelier and more patient companions. All he knows initially, though, is that things are different. The child can be counted on to cry and fuss and test the parents' resolve to follow through with the new program. Parents can be reassured that this crying will not result in any psychological damage. The advantages of good solid sleep for all family members clearly outweigh any temporary discomfort. Parents should also be aware that the number of night wakings may temporarily increase during the first few days of the program's implementation.

Devising a Plan

Parents do need to make a definite plan about how they will handle the child's crying. The plan should be drawn up and agreed upon well in advance of bedtime. Decisions made at 3 A.M. are not usually very well thought out. Everyone who deals with the child at nap or bedtime should be familiar with the plan so that a consistent approach can be achieved. Even if one parent will be primarily responsible for enacting the plan, support from the other spouse is critical to maintaining morale.

There are two basic options regarding crying. One is the infamous "cold turkey" approach in which the parents do not respond to the child no matter how long he cries. This method is very hard on both the child and the parents. In fact, parents are often unable to do this. What usually happens, as it did with Sherry's mother, is that the parent gives up after the child engages in a protracted period of crying. This teaches the child that she needs only to be persistent to get a response. Thus, her crying is reinforced rather than eliminated.

The graduated approach is much kinder to the child and the family. It involves giving the child some time to settle on his own before the parents come in to provide reassurance. The parents must agree beforehand on the length of time they can allow the child to cry without responding. Usually, this amounts to one to five minutes. Once the child is up at night, the parents must let the agreed time elapse before responding. It is important actually to monitor the interval with a timer or digital clock, because it always seems like an eternity when a child is crying.

Parents are not required to listen to the child's cries and be miserable. They can wear earplugs, run the shower, vacuum, hair dryer, or television, close the doors, or take a walk outside while waiting for the interval to elapse.

If the child is still awake after the time is up, the parent should make a brief appearance at the bedside. The purpose of the parent's visit is to reassure the child that he is not being abandoned. The parent's ministrations should be comforting but not so extensive that the child mistakes this for an after-hours playtime. The parent can pat the child's back or talk to him but should avoid taking him out of the crib. If the child has vomited, as Danny did, the bedclothes should be changed in an impassive way.

If the child continues to cry once the parent leaves, another wait of the same length of time should precede the next return visit. This pattern should be repeated, each time with a gradually longer interval, until the child goes back to sleep. For instance if the initial interval was 5 minutes, the pattern would be two 5-minute intervals, two 10-minute intervals, and as many 15-minute intervals as needed until the child falls asleep. If the child's sobs seem to be subsiding but the interval is up, it is better to wait a few extra minutes than to risk setting the child off again. This procedure needs to be employed with each night waking.

It is helpful to keep a log for the first few nights that the program is used (see Table 13.1). A log makes it easy to identify progress and spot problems. Information that should be noted includes the time the child awakened, the length of time it took until he went back to sleep, and the number of parental visits during the night.

Families often choose to start such a program on a Friday night so that they can catch up on sleep during the weekend. If the program is adhered to in a firm and consistent manner, positive results can be expected within one to two weeks.

Special Situations

Sometimes there is a need to suspend the program for a few days because of a special family occasion or an illness. The program can be resumed once the situation returns to normal.

This kind of program should be used with caution in children less than a year of age. Some infants do not sleep through the night because they are physiologically not ready to do so. Trying behavioral management with these children will be frustrating and, ultimately, unsuccessful.

Follow-up

Sherry, Danny, Lauren, and their parents are now blissfully sleeping through the night.

Sherry's mother started by purchasing a dozen extra pacifiers and strewing them around the crib. She figured that if there were more pacifiers around, Sherry could reach

89

for one when she awakened at night and comfort herself. When this didn't work, she resigned herself to putting her daughter to bed without the pacifier. Within a week, Sherry no longer awakened at night.

Danny's mother established a new bedtime ritual of cuddling and listening to music. She then placed him directly in the crib. When he cried during the night, she patted his back and said, "Good night. I love you. I'll see you in the morning." The first night she had to go to him four times. The second night was the same. She contemplated giving up but decided to continue because she had already invested two nights' work. For the next week, Danny only got up once a night for the first time in his life. By two weeks, he wasn't getting up at night at all. During this time, Mrs. Laster received confirmation of a second pregnancy. She plans to avoid inappropriate sleep onset associations with the new baby by placing him, awake, in the place where he is expected to spend the night.

Lauren's parents spoke with her about their expectation that she sleep on her own. Mr. and Mrs. Budd also discussed their intentions to work on Lauren's sleep habits with their neighbors and worked out an amicable plan. Over a few weeks, they moved from lying down with her to sitting in a chair by the bedside. Eventually, they were able to leave the room while she was awake, provided that they promised to check on her in five minutes. When they came in to see her she was, invariably, asleep.

During the daytime, the children continued to be their delightful selves. This reassured the parents that there were no ill effects attributable to the crying. The children were noted to have longer attention spans and be less easily frustrated. The parents, too, reported feeling calmer and more energetic. They emerged from this experience with a renewed sense of confidence in their abilities as parents.

90

17

NIGHT FEEDING

Angela Berry, 18 months old, always fussed at bedtime. She had a regular bedtime ritual. After dinner, she had a bath. Then her parents read a book or listened to music with her in her room. As soon as she was lifted into her crib, Angela emitted ear-shattering cries of protest. Mrs. Berry discovered that offering Angela a bottle in bed calmed her down. Angela would drink her bottle contentedly and drift off to sleep. Mrs. Berry would then return to the room later to check on Angela and retrieve the bottle.

Angela began to wake up many times during the night, asking for milk. Mrs. Berry tried to distract her but often relented and gave her a bottle out of sheer exhaustion. Angela frequently took only one or two sips and then fell back to sleep.

In the mornings, she began to get up very early. Her diaper was soaked, and she seemed uncomfortable. She was starting to develop a rash.

Mrs. Berry was confused. Why was Angela getting up so many times at night? If she was truly hungry, then why was she taking only a sip or two of her milk? With the early morning awakenings, her whole schedule seemed to be unraveling. What could she do?

For the first several months of life, feeding around the clock is normal. An infant's small stomach cannot hold enough milk to sustain her for more than three to four hours. By four to six months, most healthy babies have attained sufficient weight and stomach size to be able to lengthen the time between feedings. The middle of the night feeding is usually the first to be eliminated. Another major development that occurs at this time is the ability to string several sleep cycles together. The timing of these two events results in a baby who is able to sleep through the night.

There are exceptions to this scenario. Pediatricians sometimes advise parents to continue feeding a child at night if she is growing slowly or has serious medical problems. Some babies persist in waking at night to feed solely out of habit. There are also circumstances in which night feeders are created.

Marvin was such a child. Marvin slept through the night at two months of age. At eight months, he began waking nightly with teething pain. His parents gave him a bottle to calm him down. In a few weeks the teething problem had resolved, but Marvin was still getting up at night for a bottle.

Night feedings had developed into a habit for Marvin. His body became used to having milk at a particular time. He woke up on cue, expecting to be fed.

The situation with Angela was somewhat different. The bottle was part of her sleep onset associations. (See also Key 16.) She was used to having the bottle with her when she fell asleep. When she awakened during the night, she could not fall back to sleep unless she had the bottle with her. It was clear that she was not really hungry because she took only one or two sips of milk. The extra liquid at night increased her production of urine. The wet diapers caused the diaper rash. The discomfort of the rash, combined with the soaked diapers, prompted her early morning awakenings.

Disadvantages of Night Feedings

There are some very good reasons that Marvin's and Angela's parents would want to eliminate the night feedings. Going to bed with a bottle of milk puts the child at risk for *milk bottle cavities*. When the milk pools in the mouth for long periods of time, the sugar in the milk acts on the teeth and causes decay. The teeth then discolor, erode, and, in some cases, must be extracted. Milk may also reflux up into the eustachian tubes, which connect the upper throat and the ear, predisposing the child to middle ear infections.

Feeding at night also disrupts the body's hormonal cycles. The digestive system is supposed to be at rest during the evening. When the child feeds at night, this system becomes activated at a time when it would ordinarily not be. Other hormones, such as growth hormone, are primarily secreted during sleep. Disruption of sleep can affect the elaboration of this important growth-promoting factor.

There are personal reasons to encourage sleeping through the night as well. A child who is well rested has more energy, patience, and motivation for daytime activities. She will be a much more pleasant companion.

There are also advantages for the parents. If the child sleeps through the night, then the parents can as well. Parents who have had adequate sleep have better energy reserves to face the challenges and stresses of parenting. Wanting to start the day refreshed and with a positive attitude is not a selfish wish. It is a simple acknowledgment that energy is an essential ingredient for quality parenting.

Eliminating Night Feedings

The key to management is eliminating the feeding. First, check with the pediatrician to make sure that the feeding is not necessary for health reasons. Going over the child's growth chart can be very reassuring to parents on this point.

Several strategies can be employed to deal with night feedings. One is to stop the feedings immediately and completely. This is what Mrs. Berry decided to do. She gave Angela her last bottle of the day after dinner, so that it was no longer associated with the crib and sleep. She then sat down with Angela and explained that she was no longer going to give her any milk at night because it was going to ruin her teeth. When she placed Angela in the crib the first night of the program she said, "Now remember, Angela, no milk." As she walked out of the room Angela called out to her, "And, Mom, no juice!"

That is how a new family ritual was born. Each night mother and daughter tried to outdo each other with a listing of prohibitions that ranged from "no pear nectar" to "no champagne." When Angela cried out for milk at night, Mrs. Berry went in to see her, reminded her that she was not getting any more milk, and gave her a hug. Mrs. Berry kept the nighttime interventions brief. She wanted to reassure Angela that she was not being abandoned and satisfy herself that Angela was all right. She did not want to substitute a new habit, however, like a midnight playtime, for the night feedings. Once Angela got used to going to bed without a bottle, she stopped waking up for it during the night.

Other families might choose to handle this at a slower pace. Marvin's mother reduced the amount of milk in his bottle by 1 ounce every other night. After a week, he stopped getting up for the bottle altogether. Another way to approach this problem is to dilute the liquid progressively. Start with three-quarter strength, and in a few days change to half liquid and half water. Continue diluting until only water is being offered. The child usually does not bother getting up for water alone. If he continues to get up, then the volume reduction strategy can be implemented.

These techniques work well if they are applied firmly and consistently. This takes some effort, but a good night's rest for everyone in the family is worth it.

18

~~~~~~

COLIC

As reliable as an alarm clock, every night at six Linda started to wail, her face bright red from crying and her legs pulled up against a rigid, distended abdomen. Mr. Stanton went through his routine, checking whether she was hungry, in pain, or in need of a clean diaper. He then tried to hold her, soothe her to sleep, give her a pacifier, and play with her favorite rattle. Nothing seemed to work. This was the absolute low point of his day. He was exhausted from the myriad chores of parenting and struggling to get dinner on the table. He was looking forward to some adult conversation with his wife, who was due home from work any minute. He felt like the most incompetent parent on earth. Sometimes, he left Linda in her crib, crying, and shut himself in his room for a few minutes to escape the unrelenting and accusatory screams.

L inda's story is a typical picture of colic. She was a thriving two month old who cried for up to three hours almost every night. She had been doing this for three weeks. Colic itself is not a sleep problem, but the two conditions are associated. Understanding how colic affects sleep can help parents to care for these challenging infants.

The behavior of an infant with colic includes inconsolable crying that usually occurs in the late afternoon or evening and may last several hours. Associated features may include a red face, an arched back, and extremities that are cold to the touch. The infant's legs may be pulled up, her abdomen may be distended, and she may pass gas. This syndrome may start as early as 5 to 10 days of life and ends, in most infants, by three months. In premature babies, the onset of colic may be delayed until four to eight weeks of age. It is estimated that between 2 and 20 percent of babies have colic.

There are many theories about what causes colic but few definitive answers. Allergies, poor feeding technique, and gastrointestinal problems have been cited frequently. One persuasive theory is that colicky babies are very sensitive to the environment. They can easily be overstimulated by the sights, sounds, and experiences of normal daily caretaking. The crying is an outlet for the tension that builds up over the day.

Infants with colic are physically healthy and feed and grow well. An infant who cries and is not thriving, or has vomiting, diarrhea, constipation, or a rash, probably does not have colic. An infant with these problems should be thoroughly checked by the pediatrician.

A colicky infant is a real challenge to a parent. Mr. Stanton's experience was typical. He conscientiously checked for the most usual causes of crying—hunger, pain, and discomfort. He tried various methods to console Linda. When he was not successful in stopping her crying, he felt awful. He began to doubt his ability as a parent. Sometimes he just had to leave the room because the crying made him so miserable.

Dealing with Colic

A number of remedies can be tried with a crying infant. Some infants respond well to motion, which can be introduced by carrying the baby in a front pack or attaching a vibrating device to the crib. (See the last section of the book for ordering information.) Some babies are comforted by the combination of motion, warmth, and sound that can be experienced by sitting in an infant chair atop a clothes dryer or dishwasher. It is important always to supervise the infant closely during these activities. A lower tech way to provide warmth is a hot-water bottle under the crib sheets. Parents should check the sheets to make sure they are not too hot and remove the hot-water bottle before placing the baby in the crib.

Changes in feeding techniques have been suggested. It might be helpful to feed the baby more slowly. Some doctors believe a colicky baby should be fed small amounts of food at more frequent intervals through the day. It is very important to burp the baby often to eliminate potentially painful gas. In addition to the usual burping position, the over-the-shoulder, across-the-knee, and along-the-forearm football carry methods all have advocates.

There is a time, as Mr. Stanton discovered, when parents exhaust the list of strategies and are just too frantic to carry on any longer. It is entirely appropriate, then, to take a calming break. A frenzied parent cannot soothe a child. In fact, he will probably succeed only in communicating tension, which prolongs the crying and creates a vicious cycle. Parents should not hesitate to call in the reinforcements who have been clamoring for a chance to care for the baby. Their assistance during the baby's crying time will provide a much needed respite for the parents.

Parents should realize that sometimes a baby just has a real need to cry. They can try all their comforting maneuvers and nothing works. This is the time to remember that parental adequacy is not judged by how quickly a parent can silence an infant's cries. It is the responsiveness and caring that really count.

Parental anxiety about the baby's crying can be assuaged by a visit to the pediatrician. A normal examination can reassure parents that the baby does not have a serious illness. The crying will still be aggravating but much less worrisome.

Colic and Infant Temperament

Temperament is the link that joins colic and sleep behavior. Many babies with colic share certain characteristics, and these affect sleep. One finding is that many babies with colic tend to be very sensitive to environmental stimuli. They may be bothered, for instance, by bright light. Their need for physical stimulation is either very high or very low. Their sensitivity to the environment causes them to wake frequently during periods of light sleep. This is consistent with parental observations that these babies are not sound sleepers.

Parents can lessen some sleep disturbances by manipulating the environment. A heavy curtain or shades can block out sunlight. An infant with colic should sleep in a quiet room away from street noises and heavily trafficked areas of the house. The colicky infant tends to move around a lot at night and will undoubtedly kick off the blankets. She will be more comfortable dressed for the night in a blanket sleeper.

Children who have had colic tend to go to sleep at a later hour, to wake earlier, and to take shorter daytime naps. They have frequent night wakings even after the colic is resolved. The night wakings are due to the child's sleep onset associations, the conditions the child depends on to fall asleep.

Parents usually take an active role in settling a colicky baby to sleep. They may pat the baby's back or rock her. The child learns to depend on these maneuvers and cannot fall asleep without them. When she wakes up at night, her sleep onset associations must be restored before she can fall back to sleep.

To remedy this situation, parents must change the infant's sleep onset associations as soon as the colic resolves. This usually occurs when the child is four months old. It is important not to let poor sleep habits endure. The more fixed they become, the more difficult it is to change them. Key 16 contains information that is helpful on this issue.

The colicky infant is a challenge. Information about her sleep behavior allows parents to anticipate and understand her needs.

19

~~~~~~

HEADBANGING AND OTHER RHYTHMIC BEHAVIORS

Luis, age two years, had a very distinctive way of putting himself to sleep. He started his routine by getting up on all fours and rocking vigorously. He would then proceed to hit his forehead forcefully against the headboard of his crib. This would go on for 10 to 15 minutes until he fell asleep. Luis banged his head before his daytime nap as well. Although Luis seemed fine during the day and was developing normally, Mr. and Mrs. Cruz felt that something must be wrong to account for this strange behavior. Their greatest concern was that the banging, which had been going on for a year, would lead to brain damage in their son.

Luis exhibits many of the typical features associated with headbanging and body rocking. Headbanging, body rocking, and head rolling are characterized as *rhythmic behaviors*. Rhythmic behaviors are seen in 10 to 30 percent of normal children between one and five years of age.

Rhythmic behaviors emerge early in life. Body rocking starts at about 6 months and headbanging and head rolling at approximately 9 months. These behaviors rarely begin after 18 months. Some infants body rock first and then add headbanging to their repertoire a few weeks later. Rhythmic behaviors can persist for weeks, months, or years. They usually stop within 18 months of onset and are rarely seen after age four.

Of all young children, 20 percent engage in body rocking at some point during the day. This often occurs while they are listening to music, but 10 percent do so at bedtime. They may rock on all fours, as Luis did, or rock while sitting up. Rocking may occur alone or in combination with headbanging. Body rocking is equally common in boys and girls.

Headbanging and head rolling are noted in approximately five percent of young children. Headbanging is seen three times more often in boys than in girls. Headbanging can be done in a number of ways. The child can sit up and let his head fall backward against the headboard or bang his head while up on all fours. Some children lie on their stomachs, raise themselves up off the mattress, and then allow themselves to flop down. Head rolling usually consists of a side-to-side motion with the child lying on his back. Headbanging may also occur in conjunction with head rolling.

Rhythmic behaviors are most often observed at bedtime. They usually go on for 10 to 20 minutes but can last up to two hours. They can also be seen when the child is drowsy before a nap, after a nighttime waking, in the morning as he wakes, or even during sleep.

The cause of these behaviors is not known. One suggestion is that they emerge as a way of managing the pain of teething. This explanation does not really account for the persistence of these behaviors over time. An association has been noted between the onset of rhythmic behaviors and major developmental advances. A theory has

102

been put forth that rhythmic behaviors are an outlet for the tensions generated by developmental challenges. Another explanation is that these behaviors are comforting to the child and promote sleep.

Rhythmic behaviors in developmentally appropriate infants and toddlers are normal. They stop on their own and do not require active treatment. Some children get bumps and bruises from superficial bleeding in the skin. Brain injuries with this type of behavior are extremely unlikely because of the protection afforded by the bony skull.

Handling Rhythmic Behaviors

Many parents are nonetheless distressed by these behaviors. Those frustrated at the prospect of simply waiting it out may want to employ some of the following suggestions.

- One option is to provide the child with more rhythmic stimulation during the day, such as using the swings at the playground or riding a hobbyhorse. These outlets during the day may lessen the need for rhythmic behaviors at night. Playing music with a strong beat may also serve as a substitute for the child's own rocking.
- One of the problems with body rocking is the noise and damage that occur as the crib is propelled around the room. This can be alleviated by removing the mattress from the crib and placing it on the floor.
- Moving the mattress to the middle of the room may also work for the child who bangs his head on the headboard. An ingenious child does not let this deter him, however, and simply moves the mattress against the wall and bangs there. Padding the crib is another strategy.

The presence of rhythmic behaviors has serious implications in certain situations. Greater concern about these

103

behaviors is warranted if they begin after 18 months of age or recur in an older child. Children with developmental problems, such as autism, mental retardation, and blindness, often engage in rhythmic behaviors. These children require the help of a specialist to manage the behaviors effectively.

Older children use headbanging as an attention-getting device. It is sometimes difficult to believe that a child would resort to such drastic behavior. Parents should suspect this if they discover, for instance, that the child never bangs his head at rest time at school or when he sleeps at a friend's house.

A child employs headbanging because it effectively commands adult attention. Parents find it difficult to ignore a behavior they consider unusual or potentially harmful. Once the child realizes how powerful a tool headbanging is, his motivation to do it increases.

To break this cycle, parents must do two things. One is to ignore the headbanging. The child responds by stopping the headbanging when he sees that it no longer brings immediate attention.

The next step is to try to understand why the child is seeking more attention. Parents can brainstorm with each other, friends, relatives, or the child's teacher in searching for an answer to this question. The child's pediatrician is also a good resource.

The challenge for parents is to provide additional attention for appropriate behavior during the daytime. The bedtime ritual should also be reexamined. Perhaps it needs to be updated to match the child's developmental progress. Key 7 contains a number of innovative ideas.

Older children may also headbang or rock when they are anxious. They may be concerned about a family problem, such as marital discord or a serious illness. They may be fearful because of scary thoughts or fantasies that surface when they are alone at night. The rocking or banging may be their way of banishing these uncomfortable feelings.

It is important to uncover the source of these feelings. The child may open up to the parents or a professional counselor. The child can be taught relaxation techniques to use at night (see Key 7) in place of rhythmic behaviors.

Follow-up

Mr. and Mrs. Cruz spoke to Luis's pediatrician about his behavior. They were reassured that headbanging is a normal behavior in their son's age group and would not lead to brain damage. They were also told that rhythmic behaviors usually subside before age three. Mr. and Mrs. Cruz were relieved to hear that Luis was healthy and normal, but they were frustrated that there was no way to stop the behaviors more quickly. They were elated, one month later, when the headbanging and rocking came to a stop on its own.

20

CURTAIN CALL
SYNDROME

"Dad, my throat's dry."

Mr. Lee looked up from his newspaper in surprise. His three-year-old daughter, Nancy, stood before him with a forlorn expression on her face.

"Nancy, I tucked you in just a minute ago and everything was fine."

"Yes, I know, but now I'm thirsty," she whined, "You don't want me to die of thirst, do you?"

This scene, with variations, was performed nightly at the Lee household. Nancy had an established bedtime of 8 P.M. Before bed, she had a snack. Then she listened to some stories or a tape. Finally, she got a good-night kiss. Nancy was very cooperative about this routine. Immediately after Mr. and Mrs. Lee returned to the living room, however, they heard the sound of little footsteps. They were always amazed at how quickly Nancy appeared. It was as if she had just turned around and followed them out of her room.

Her requests were endless. She was hungry, then thirsty. The room was too hot or too cold, too noisy, or too quiet. She had to go to the bathroom, have one more kiss, or deliver an emergency message that could not wait until morning.

One night the Lees, trying to anticipate Nancy's every need, placed all the items she had ever requested on her

106

bedside table. They provided a cup of water, dry cereal, tissues, a flashlight, a clock, and a photograph of the family. When Nancy came out that night the Lees were stupified. What had they forgotten?

"Why am I the only one in the family who has to sleep alone?" Nancy asked. Nancy's mother reminded her of her vast menagerie of stuffed animals. "Yes, but they're not alive," Nancy replied.

Nancy Lee's behavior is a classic example of the curtain call syndrome. Children at this age find it difficult to separate from their parents at the end of the day. They are reluctant to leave the exciting world of activity and achievement. Their requests for drinks, hugs, and trips to the bathroom are not bona fide necessities but stalling tactics. The more inventive the child is, the more time she can buy herself with her parents.

Parents are thrust into a terrible dilemma. They worry about whether the child is truly hungry or thirsty. They feel guilty about the possibility of turning down a legitimate request. They are concerned that ignoring the child's pleas will damage her sense of security.

Working parents are especially vulnerable to this gambit. They are already under stress about how the child's needs are met during the day when they are not at home. Not to respond at night adds another layer of guilt. There may also be some parental ambivalence about the child's bedtime. Working parents are always looking for ways to increase the amount of time they spend with their child. When the child appears in the living room, claiming that she is not a bit tired, there is a real temptation to abandon the rules and enjoy additional time together. A parent who is alone at night may welcome the child's company and subtly encourage this sort of behavior. Parents who are not getting along well may also prefer that the child be present so that they do not have to confront their own problems.

Parents need to understand the consequences of their actions. When they accede to the child's requests, whatever their motivation, they reinforce the child's behavior. The child learns that these requests bring her the parental attention she desires. She then sets her imagination to develop a litany of demands to perpetuate the situation.

Managing the Curtain Call Syndrome

Effective management of the curtain call syndrome starts with the bedtime routine. The goal is to make bedtime the pleasant culmination of an enjoyable day, not a banishment. This can be achieved if the bedtime routine is leisurely, fun, and attuned to the child's needs. It is ideal if both parents can be involved. All other chores and obligations should be set aside. Being with the child should be the sole focus. Sufficient time should be set aside for these activities so that the child does not feel as if she's being herded off. A child should be encouraged to bring a stuffed animal or special blanket to bed with her to ease the transition.

Parents should ask the child if she's had enough to eat and drink. It should be stressed that this is her last chance for food until morning, because once she's in bed the kitchen is closed. Parents should also make sure that the child has gone to the bathroom and brushed her teeth, thus eliminating two other common reasons for curtain calls.

Parents should discuss their concerns about the stalling behavior directly with the child. She should understand that popping out of bed interferes with her getting enough sleep. She should be informed that if she leaves her room after she is tucked in, she will be brought back promptly. To provide the child with an incentive for compliance, a sticker chart can be set up. The child earns a star or sticker for each night she goes to bed without a curtain call. Parents may wish to offer a special treat if the child gains several stars in a row.

Setting Limits

The next step requires parents to set and enforce limits. The simplest stance is to, without fail, return the child promptly to bed each time she performs a curtain call. It is very important to escort the child back with a minimum of drama and emotion. Otherwise, this becomes a game and the child is tempted to pop out just to see how the parent will react.

Some parents feel uncomfortable being this inflexible. They would just as soon fulfill a simple request for another hug. This way they don't have to turn the child down; they can avoid unpleasantness, and the whole situation can be resolved in the time it would have taken to march the child back to bed anyway. Parents who take this stance need to be clear about how many curtain calls they will allow and which kinds of requests will be honored. If they can enforce their precepts firmly and consistently, this approach also works. A family who wants to use this method should budget extra time for the curtain call when setting the child's bedtime. If the child is in bed 10 minutes earlier, for instance, the time for the curtain call will not encroach upon the time she really needs for sleep.

Sometimes the routine of marching the child back to bed scores of times really starts to amuse her. Soon the process degenerates into a frenzied chasing game. When this occurs, a switch in strategy is necessary. The next time the child appears, the parents should simply ignore her.

When the child realizes that she is no longer getting any attention, she will try a new tactic. This will involve such ingenious actions as standing in front of the television, sprawling across the book that the parent is trying to read, or throwing piles of cancelled checks and bank statements around like confetti. It is very difficult for the parent to maintain composure in this situation, but it is essential. Any glimmer of recognition or amusement is interpreted by the child as a sign of encouragement. If the parent can hold out, this situation resolves by the child either returning to bed by herself or, more likely, falling asleep at the parent's side.

Don't Fence Me in

Some parents try to curb curtain calls by forcibly preventing the child from leaving her room. This is a controversial strategy. People who support it believe that it is an effective way to back up a household rule. People who oppose this practice believe that it is too harsh and might result in a backlash of more fears and sleep problems. If this method will be used, the room must be thoroughly child-proofed. Parents must ensure the safety of a child who may be angry and out of control when locked in her room.

Another approach is to hold the door closed. Parents should explain to the child that the privilege of having the door open is earned by her staying in bed. If, after a minute of door closing, the child has not returned to bed, the parent should enter and tuck her in again. If she jumps out again, the door could be held for a slightly longer time. For the first night, five minutes should be the maximum time for a single door closing. Parents can repeat the five-minute door closings as many times as necessary until the child stays in bed. This process can then be followed on succeeding nights with increasing time intervals.

Increasing Positive Attention

One other factor that should be examined in a child with the curtain call syndrome is the kind of attention she receives during the day. If the child does not have enough time with the parents during the day, the addition of even just a 20-minute one-on-one play period can make an enormous difference. This is a time to set aside all adult concerns, get down on the floor, and play something of the child's own choosing. It may be worthwhile to get up a bit earlier and do this first thing in the morning. It really gets the day off to a special start.

The curtain call syndrome is an impressive example of the child's ingenuity. It is easily handled by parents who understand the child's motivation and are able to enforce clear and consistent limits.

21

~~~~~~

THE EARLY RISER

"Hi, Mom, I'm ready to go swimming now." Ms. Glass opened her eyes and marveled at her four-year-old daughter, Jessie. Jessie had managed to dress herself in her favorite rainbow bathing suit, buckle her sandals, and find her pail and shovel. Her beach towel with the dinosaurs was draped over her shoulder. Everything seemed to be in order, yet Ms. Glass felt somewhat uneasy. Her eyes peered at the digital clock on her night table. The bright red numbers were unmistakable. It was 4:30 A.M. Another day with the early riser had begun.

C hildren who get up early can be divided into two major categories. The first group consists of children who awaken before they have completed their nightly sleep requirement. The second consists of children who get up early after getting an adequate amount of sleep during the night. The reasons for early rising and the approaches that can be used to deal with it are the subject of this chapter.

Waking Too Early

The child who awakens prematurely fails to complete the last sleep cycle of the night. The last several sleep cycles before morning consist predominantly of light sleep. Any environmental stimulus—the sunlight streaming through the curtains, traffic noise from the street, or a person in the household moving about while getting ready for work—can disrupt this type of sleep. A child may be bothered by hunger pangs or a wet diaper. Early waking can also be prompted when the child has one of the brief awakenings that normally take place between sleep cycles. As she checks her surroundings, she may notice that it is light out. Since she associates daylight with morning, she may have difficulty going back to sleep.

Another commonly offered explanation for early rising is the notion that the child does not need much sleep. There are children who can function well on less than 9 to 10 hours of sleep per night, but these children are quite rare. The average sleep requirements for children of different ages are listed in Table 5.1 (page 30).

Early morning awakening can be a function of the child's daily schedule. A five year old who goes to bed at 7 P.M. may have gotten enough sleep by 5:30 A.M. A later waking time can be achieved, but only at the cost of a later bedtime. The family must decide which arrangement best fits their needs. Shifting the child's schedule can be accomplished by delaying the bedtime by 10 minutes every few nights. The child should respond by rising a bit later with each change. This process can be continued until the family reaches a satisfactory balance between sleep and wake times.

The child's nap schedule can also be a factor in early morning awakening. A child who naps excessively during the day has a reduced need for sleep at night. Early morning waking is a consequence of this arrangement.

The Lark

The second type of early riser wakes well rested and ready to start the day. This kind of person is called a *lark*. Larks simply function best in the morning. This is the time that they are most cheerful, energetic, and clear thinking. Being a lark is great, except if all the other family members are night owls.

Dealing with the Early Riser

Determining the cause of the early rising is central to its management. The first item that must be assessed is the sufficiency of the child's sleep time. Inadequate sleep should be suspected if the child consistently gets less sleep than the average for her age according to the sleep chart (page 30). The child's behavior can provide another clue. A tired child is often cranky and difficult in the late afternoons and early evenings. Other manifestations of sleep deprivation include a short attention span, lack of patience, low frustration level, and overactivity.

This kind of early riser needs to return to sleep in the early morning. Troubleshooting in the child's room may reveal what is disturbing her sleep and promoting the early morning awakenings. Heavy curtains or window blinds can be used to block out sunlight. A white noise machine or a vaporizer can mask sounds from the street or other parts of the house. Double diapering at night may make the child more comfortable.

Some parents accommodate the early riser by inviting her into their bed for the last sleep cycle of the night. This does not eliminate the early rising but may enable everyone to get another hour of sleep. Many families find that they enjoy starting the day together.

This approach requires firm limits to work well. Parents must decide at what time the child is welcome in their bed. If they do not establish a firm rule, the child's natural tendency will be to wake progressively earlier to spend more time with them. If this process is left unchecked, the child eventually ends up sleeping with the parents for the entire night.

A similar strategy can be used with the hungry early riser. Juice or a bowl of dry cereal can be left out to quell

114

the child's hunger until morning, with the proviso that she return to bed after her snack. Parents should be aware of the consequences of their actions. Providing these snacks reinforces the child's early wakings. Parents must be clear about how far they are willing to go to accommodate the child's appetite. Without firm limits, the child's requests will escalate. She will then want more than one snack, more exotic fare, or permission to use the microwave. Parents need to decide whether they will provide one easy-to-manage snack or insist that the child wait until breakfast.

The approach is different if the child is a lark. Since a lark is well rested and ready to start the day, it is pointless to send her back to bed. The child should be made aware that, although she is up, other people are still asleep and their rights need to be respected.

Starting the Day

One way to reinforce this idea is to provide a clear signal that indicates the official start of the day. The child can be given a clock radio or digital clock and instructed to play quietly without waking other family members until the music starts or the clock reads six.

Parents should be specific about the activities that are permissible in the early morning hours. A special collection of appropriate playthings, including puzzles, books, markers, and paper, can be set aside. The child may be entertained by television or a video. Parents should remember to set the volume control at a suitable level the night before. The kitchen and other areas where play could prove noisy or dangerous should be off-limits.

Many early risers wake their parents with the complaint that they are lonely. If there is another early riser in the household, this person makes an ideal playmate. Some families provide their early riser with a goldfish or another kind of pet for company.

115

Some children cannot be without adult supervision in the morning. Parents may choose to share this responsibility, especially on weekend mornings. The dual advantage is that the parents have the opportunity for both extra sleep and individual time with the child.

Some families with larks choose to start their day early and compensate by ending it early, too. This is particularly easy to do with young children, who do not have to conform to the worldly schedules of nursery programs and school. Rising early provides a head start to the day, with some very real advantages. The local 24-hour supermarket is a lot less crowded at 7 A.M. than later in the day. If dinner is prepared early, the late afternoon can be a lot less hectic.

This kind of schedule is actually a boon to working families. Parents can spend time with the child at the start of the day, when patience and energy levels are high. This also eliminates the pressure of having to squeeze in playtime at the end of the day, when everyone is really too worn out to enjoy it.

There are challenges and compensations to living with an early riser. Sunrise can be a wonderful part of the day.

Follow-up

Ms. Glass baked a batch of brownies and packed the picnic basket. She and Jessie arrived at the beach at just about the same time as the lifeguards.

22

THE CHILD WHO WON'T STAY IN BED

Jamal, age four, had a beautiful bedroom. It was painted purple, his favorite color. Posters of his beloved sea creatures, gifts from his grandmother, adorned the walls. Mr. and Mrs. Washington took Jamal to the furniture store when they bought his bed. He even selected his own sheets—blue with puffy white clouds, yellow stars, and silvery moons. It was a lovely, cheerful room, and no one in the family could figure out why Jamal never spent a single night there!

Every morning, his parents awoke to find Jamal, curled in a tight ball, fast asleep at the foot of their bed. They were both sound sleepers, so they never heard him enter the room. Jamal's behavior puzzled them. He did not appear upset at night, as if he had had a scary dream. He never voiced fears about his room. In fact, he played happily there in the daytime. He was cheerful and energetic during the day and made an excellent adjustment to nursery school.

The Washingtons felt Jamal should sleep in his own room. They consulted with Jamal's pediatrician and formulated a plan to change Jamal's sleeping place.

There are several factors to consider when a child refuses to sleep in his own room.

Making the Room Comfortable

First, make sure the child regards his room as a comfortable place. The Washingtons did this by involving their son in the selection of furnishings. Jamal was able to choose colors and patterns that appealed to him. These decisions made Jamal feel important and grown up. Mr. Washington made a special contribution to the room-decorating project. He helped Jamal make two signs to hang on the door to his room. One read "Jamal's Place" and the other read "Please knock." The Washingtons also made sure that the room had only positive associations for their son by never using it as a place for punishment.

Sometimes a room that looks fine during the day becomes threatening at night. If parents spend time in the child's room after dark, they may notice that the furniture casts scary shadows. This problem can be eliminated by removing the objects or changing their position.

The Bedtime Ritual

The next element is the bedtime ritual. (See also Key 6.) This should be a loving prelude to sleep. Parents should make sure that they allow sufficient time for all necessary activities, including quiet play, a snack, a trip to the bathroom, changing into pajamas, toothbrushing, reading stories, listening to music, and goodnight hugs and kisses. This is a lot to accomplish in a short time. If these activities are rushed, the child suspects that the parents are dumping him to get on to more exciting pastimes and he reacts by actively resisting sleep. If the ritual has not gone on long enough to allow the child to relax, he may truly be unable to fall asleep.

Adequate Daytime Attention

Next, consider the amount of attention the child receives during the daytime. Jamal's parents wondered if his behavior at night meant that he was not getting enough attention during the day. They decided to alter their after-dinner schedule to include more playtime with Jamal. Instead of clearing the dishes directly after dinner, they used that time for an activity of Jamal's choosing. Sometimes they played with his farm animals. Other times they painted or played a card game. They were also advised to carry out these activities in Jamal's room. Conducting the bedtime ritual in the child's room builds up an association between sleep and the place where it should occur. With their new routine in place, the Washingtons noticed a marked decrease in resistance at bedtime.

Implementing the Plan

Mr. and Mrs. Washington spoke directly with Jamal about the importance of sleeping in his bed for the whole night. They explained how a good night's rest gave him the energy he needed to learn and play in school every day. They suggested that he just turn over and go back to sleep if he woke up during the night. He was promised a new sticker in the morning for each night spent entirely in his own room. They also informed Jamal that he would be carried right back to his room if he visited his parent's bed during the night. They gave Jamal an opportunity to express his feelings. It was important to know whether he had any fears or concerns that had been overlooked.

The Washingtons knew that keeping their promise to return Jamal to his room would be a challenge. How would they ever be able to get him out of their bed when they never even heard him get into it?

They thought about ways of keeping Jamal in his room. They dismissed a gate: they knew it would be no match for his climbing skills. They rejected locking his door or barricading it with furniture. They felt that Jamal would become panicky if he could not get out of his room. They did not want their son to have negative associations with "Jamal's Place."

The Washington's plan was to attach a set of sleigh bells to their bedroom door, which would ring as soon as

Jamal entered the room. Then one of the parents would get up and walk Jamal back to his room. They understood the importance of applying the new rule firmly and consistently so that Jamal would not doubt their resolve.

For three nights, Mr. and Mrs. Washington felt like a ferry service transporting Jamal back to his room innumerable times each night. Jamal thought this was hilarious. As soon as he was put back in bed, he would jump out and race down the hall to his parents' room. Sometimes he even made it there before they did. The Washingtons were exhausted and disgusted. The situation was even worse than before they started. At least, then, they were getting a full night's sleep.

Troubleshooting

On Sunday morning, four days into the program, the Washingtons shared a pot of strong coffee and analyzed their progress. They knew they had done well in terms of being firm and consistent in their commitment to the plan, but this was obviously not sufficient. Further discussion led them to understand two key weaknesses.

Escorting Jamal back to bed had become an elaborate kind of game. Jamal loved the new sport of racing his parents around the apartment after midnight. The angrier they got, the more amusing a show they put on. Jamal was also so revved up from all the activity that he genuinely found it difficult to fall back to sleep. The Washingtons decided to respond by returning Jamal to bed in the most nonchalant manner possible. In this way, they would stop rewarding his leaving bed by running the midnight marathon.

The Washingtons also realized that the key was not just physically returning Jamal to his bedroom but getting him to fall back to sleep there. They thought that if they sat with him, perhaps Jamal would settle down and go back to sleep. They were unenthusiastic about the prospect of spending the night in a chair, but they felt that at least Jamal would be sleeping in the right room.

Following Through

The first night it was Mr. Washington's turn. When Jamal got up, Mr. Washington silently escorted him back to his room. Mr. Washington stretched out on a chair and fell asleep. In the morning, he had a backache but was elated when he realized that Jamal had spent the night in his own room.

The next night, Mrs. Washington decided to stay in Jamal's room, just until she was sure he was asleep. This did not work out too well. Jamal got up, noticed that his mother was not in the chair, and came looking for her.

Then the family evolved a better plan. The "escorting" parent would return with Jamal to his room and put on his favorite tape. At first, Jamal insisted that the parent stay for the whole first side. Eventually, they worked out a compromise. The parent would leave the room after the first song and return to check on Jamal in five minutes, provided that he stayed in bed. The first few nights Jamal was awake at the five-minute check. His parents faithfully kept to their side of the bargain, and within a week, Jamal was asleep by the time a parent came to check on him.

Jamal enjoyed picking out his reward sticker each morning and glowed with the praise he received from his parents. Mr. and Mrs. Washington were proud that they persevered and resolved a family problem with positive results for all concerned.

23

MONSTERS AND OTHER STRANGERS IN THE NIGHT

Toby was a boisterous and outgoing five year old. In the playground, he was always found on the top rung of the jungle gym—unless he was trying to break a speed record on his bicycle. He enjoyed meeting different kinds of people and exploring new places.

It was puzzling, then, to Mr. and Mrs. Hughes that their son underwent such a dramatic transformation at night. "I can't sleep in my room. There are monsters there," Toby complained. Every night Mrs. Hughes, armed with her flashlight, made a diligent search of Toby's room. She pronounced it free of monsters, but this did not seem to comfort Toby. Getting Toby to bed at night became a major battle as he demanded more stories, more hugs, and countless glasses of water.

C hildren who seem perfectly well adjusted during the day, like Toby, can have profound fears at night. During the daytime there is a lot of stimulation to occupy the mind. At night, when the distractions are stripped away, fears can surface. Children are less well equipped to deal with their fears at night. They tend to regress, or act more babyish, at the close of the day. They have less control over their thoughts, feelings, and urges. When the vivid imagination of a five year old goes unchecked at night, it is easy to see how monsters could take up residence under the bed.

Age-Related Fears

Specific fears are linked to the developmental issues children face at particular ages. For an infant, bedtime means separation from the people who nurture him. Separation may be heightened for the child who spends long periods of time apart from his parents during the day.

The toddler years are a constant tug-of-war between opposite urges. The child strives to control more of his behavior: dress himself, feed himself, use the toilet, and verbalize feelings rather than bite or pull hair. Occasionally, these demands become overwhelming and the toddler reverts to being clingy, stubborn, and dependent.

These opposing forces act on sleep behavior as well. The toddler knows what is expected at bedtime but is reluctant to leave the exciting adult world. He wants to be independent at night, but at the same time, he wants to be sure that there will always be someone to take care of him and to love him. He worries about how he is handling the new experiences of using the toilet, going to nursery school, and being a sibling.

Preschoolers show increased mastery over their bodies and their everyday experiences. A primary task is to develop a sense of self. One aspect involves learning to control aggressive feelings. The objects of preschoolers' fears in the external world—noisy, violent, uncontrolled creatures—mirror their inner struggles for control. Preschoolers may also be fearful of shadows and the dark.

School-aged children have entered a wider world that includes peers and teachers in addition to family members.

123

They become aware of serious issues, such as academic achievement, illness, and death. Realities in the child's environment—news reports of violence, a parental separation, a move to a new home, a change in schools, a recent robbery, or a frightening television show—can prompt fears. Children often worry about the remote possibility of harm befalling their loved ones. They also fear not being able to measure up to their peers.

Understanding Children's Fears

The most important step in aiding a child with fears is to understand what fuels them. Monsters are merely the form given to uncomfortable feelings. If the source of the feelings is not addressed, the monsters can never be eradicated. This is why cosmetic approaches alone, such as searching the room, are seldom effective.

In a positive way, monsters can be seen as a clear and urgent call for help. Although parents might dismiss a request for one more story or another bowl of ice cream, they cannot very well send a child back to a room inhabited by a hideous purple monster with large fangs and green scales. Monsters elicit empathy, reassurance, and promises of protection from the parents, which is precisely what the child needs.

Parents need to understand the motivation for the child's changed bedtime behavior. When children have fears at night, they react by trying to put off sleep as long as possible. As Toby did, they come up with millions of excuses to avoid the time when they must be alone with their feelings. The bedtime ritual becomes longer. Parents, not surprisingly, feel impatient and manipulated.

If the fears began quite suddenly, it is reasonable to suspect a particular incident, such as a disturbing television show or video, as the source. Families who screen their children's television viewing should remember that a child may be exposed to unsuitable material at a friend's house.

Parents need to talk with the child about his fears. A discussion about fears is best left for the daytime, when the child can think about them logically rather than emotionally. The point of this discussion is to search for constructive solutions. It is important to avoid simply dismissing the fears as babyish. This only makes the child feel worse. What the child needs now is full parental support.

Managing Children's Fears

Parents should count on spending extra time with a fearful child at bedtime. They should seek to assure the child that he is safe and protected. Parents must find a way to provide reassurance without substantiating the child's monster fantasy. An extensive search of the room, like the one done by Mrs. Hughes, can actually escalate a child's fears. The harder the parent looks, the more credence this gives the child's beliefs and the more scared he becomes. "Wow, so Mom really believes it, too," the child thinks. When the monster is not found, the child feels that the parent did not work hard enough and has failed to protect him. A quick scan of the room is sufficient to communicate the parent's faith in the child and the commitment to safeguard him.

Other strategies can be employed to help a child master this experience. Mrs. Hughes furnished Toby with an imaginary can of monster spray to be used just in case he sighted anything. A flashlight can be used in much the same way. Some children select a ferocious stuffed animal to keep watch over them while they are asleep. Some enjoy sharing a room with a sibling or a pet.

Children who are afraid of the dark can have a night-light in the room. Other options are to leave a light on in a closet or adjoining hallway. The room light can be attached to a dimmer switch and turned down as the child's comfort level permits. Photosensitive stars and moons can be fixed to the walls or ceiling. They provide an attractive glow for a few minutes after the lights are turned off. Special glow-in-the-dark markers are available for families who prefer to design their own stickers.

Sometimes the glare of headlights or the beam from a street lamp casts a disturbing shadow in the child's room. It is worthwhile sitting with the child and having him point out what bothers him. An opaque curtain can block out offending light. The furniture can be rearranged so that the shadow is no longer in the child's line of vision. Moving the furniture should be done only once. A nightly ritual of shifting things around does not contribute to a child's feeling of security.

Books are also very useful in helping a child with his fears. They demonstrate to the child that he is not alone in having these types of feelings. Some books, which depict children and their personal monsters, are a perfect point of departure for a discussion of the child's particular fears. The child may want to describe how his monster differs from the one in the book. Drawing the monster and then shrinking it on a copy machine or cutting it into infinitesimal pieces and throwing it in the garbage are other ways to gain control. Books are also helpful in providing a variety of models for coping. The child may decide to emulate his favorite book character or become inspired to devise his own strategy. A list of pertinent titles can be found at the end of this book.

Usually, parental support and reassurance are sufficient to enable a child to deal with nighttime fears.

Occasionally, fears mushroom and affect daytime functioning as well. The child clings, unwilling even to play in the bedroom alone, and is panicked at night. This is when professional intervention is needed. Parents should also consider professional help when the child shows a reluctance to discuss his fears with the family.

24

~~~~~~

NIGHTMARES

"There were pirates and they had swords and they were chasing me," sobbed five-year-old Lizzie. Mr. Taylor smoothed his daughter's hair and held her close. "It's only a dream," he said, "just make believe." "Yes, I know, but I'm still really scared," Lizzie replied and burst into tears.

Nightmares are, very simply, bad dreams. As with all dreams, nightmares occur during REM sleep. They are most likely to occur in the early morning hours when most REM sleep is concentrated.

Dreaming is one of the ways a child processes the emotional conflicts that she experiences each day. Parents can gain unique insights into a child's world if they take note of the contents of her dreams.

Dreams and Development

Little is known about dreaming in infancy because babies are unable to issue verbal reports. Parents can surmise from their one year old's behavior and verbalizations that she's had a dream, even though she will be unable to label it as such. She may seem upset after she awakens, as if she still feels threatened by something. This is because she lacks the perspective to understand that the dream is over.

Two year olds begin to develop the concept of a dream but may still have difficulty distinguishing the boundary between dreaming and reality. Issues of separation, based on real-life events, figure prominently in their dreams. This includes such situations as staying with a new babysitter or coping with a parent's absence because of business commitments or hospitalization.

By the time a child reaches the age of three, she can clearly tell the difference between a dream and real life. Three to five year olds focus on modulating their aggressive and sexual feelings. They are learning about appropriate limits for their behavior. They are also working through the phase of competition with the same-sex parent. This is the peak age for nightmares. Preschoolers' nightmares are populated by animals and other scary figures that play out some of these control issues. Two common plots involve the child being chased and the child having difficulty finding her way home.

Children have a decreased frequency of nightmares during the elementary school years. This is because the issues that found expression in nightmares are largely resolved by this time. In addition, children of this age have evolved other mechanisms to cope with conflicts.

Nightmares increase again with the stresses of adolescence.

Some children must cope with family-based pressures in addition to developmental pressures. Children who frequently witness arguing or domestic violence at home are more prone to nightmares. Exposure to scary books, television shows, or videos can induce nightmares. Monitoring and reducing this kind of input can decrease the frequency of nightmares.

Coping with Nightmares

Occasional nightmares are an inevitable by-product of growing up. Parents should be prepared with a plan to deal with them when they occur.

The first priority after a nightmare is to comfort the child. This is a time when even the most standoffish child is receptive to close physical contact. Older children benefit from verbal reassurances in addition to a hug. The main message to convey is that the child is safe and cannot be harmed.

It is important to clarify, as Lizzie's father did, that the experience was a dream. Labeling the experience puts the incident in context. This is especially critical for the child who is not completely alert and is still terrified that her pursuers are lurking in the room. Labeling is also helpful for the young child who is just starting to understand the difference between fantasy and reality.

Labeling must be done with the utmost tact. Although the experience was "only a dream," the emotional reactions are quite real. The scary feelings must be acknowledged and assuaged before the child can return to sleep.

It is not necessary that a child recount the events of the dream in detail. For some children, however, this process is integral to their mastering the experience. The specifics may be enlightening for parents who are searching for inciting factors in the child's daily life. Some children don't want to talk about the dream until the morning, when the immediacy of the situation has passed. Children who are visually oriented may prefer to draw a picture of the nightmare. Other children find it too threatening to relive the situation at all, or they have a poor recollection of the details.

After a nightmare, the child may want a parent to keep her company for a while until she can go back to sleep. Some parents allow a child who has had a nightmare to sleep in their bed or in their room. A light left on in the room can also be comforting.

Children sometimes fear that the nightmare will resume where it left off, once they return to sleep. One strategy is to suggest to the child that she has a "dream control center" in her brain. She can be reminded to flip off the bad dream switch and change to a new dream channel before going back to sleep.

Daytime Strategies

Parents can best help a child deal with her fears if they know, specifically, what the fears are. A discussion about the child's fears is more appropriately conducted during the daytime than just before going to bed.

One way to deal with an infant's fears around separation is to play games like peek-a-boo. This kind of game reinforces the idea that disappearing objects always return.

A young child may have difficulty articulating her fears. In this situation, books can be an invaluable resource. There are wonderful books that deal specifically with dreams and nightmares. There are also some very special books that deal with fears of other sorts. The value of books in this context is that the child feels understood, is moved to examine her own feelings, and is provided with models for coping. A list of suitable books can be found in the last section of this book.

With an older child, a specific fear may be elicited easily. The discussion should then focus on a constructive way to handle it.

If a child is older than six and still having frequent nightmares or has fears that impede daily functioning, professional help should be sought. The child's pediatrician can make a referral to an appropriate professional.

Before Bed

The bedtime ritual should be reexamined to make sure that no scary elements have been inadvertently included. A discussion of dreams can be part of the ritual. The child can suggest pleasant things that she'd like to dream about and then be encouraged to focus on these images as she goes to sleep.

A "dream machine" can be created from an empty carton covered with foil, bits of used wrapping paper, or fabric scraps. Dials and gauges can be painted or made of buttons. As part of the bedtime ritual, the child can use the machine to select her dream. Should she have a nightmare, exchanging the bad dream for a new selection can be part of the process of going back to bed.

Could It Be a Night Terror?

Nightmares can sometimes be confused with night terrors. It is important to distinguish between these two entities because they need to be handled differently.

Night terrors occur during the first part of the night. The child may talk, cry out, or moan but is not really awake. She may be thrashing about in bed or sitting upright. She does not appear to recognize her parents and may even push them away if they approach to console her. The episode resolves on its own and the child easily returns to sleep. In the morning, she has no memory of the event and is not able to recall any dream. For more on this topic, see Key 27.

There are several instances in which nightmares and night terrors can be confused. Parents may hear the moaning of a night terror and assume that the child is

132

talking about a dream. They may interpret her rejection of physical comforting as a lingering fear induced by a dream. When the child actually wakes as the terror ends, she may not return to sleep in the classically easy way if she is alarmed by the sight of two anxious parents at her bedside.

If parents are unsure about whether the child is having a nightmare or a night terror, the best strategy is to wait and observe the child. If the child returns to sleep on her own, the episode was most likely a night terror. Waiting before intervening does not harm a child who has had a nightmare. A child awakening from a nightmare can be confused and disoriented as well as frightened. A moment or two of quiet enables her to get her bearings. She is then able to fully appreciate her parents' comforting maneuvers.

Nightmares are a normal part of growing up. They serve as a reminder of how children actively deal with their fears and anxieties. Parents can assist in this process by providing safe contexts for the expression of feelings. When the inevitable nightmare occurs, there is no match for a parent's special blend of love and support.

~~~~~~

25

SLEEP, ILLNESS, AND MEDICATION

Various acute and chronic illnesses have an impact on sleep. Understanding these relationships assists parents in caring for their children.

Diaper rash results when the skin is irritated by prolonged contact with urine or feces. This situation is exacerbated at night, when diapers are changed less frequently than they are during the daytime. Soaked diapers or wet bedclothes lead to discomfort and promote waking, particularly in the early morning.

Several steps can be taken to lessen the problems associated with diaper rash. Feeding the infant during the night should be avoided because it leads to increased urine production. A skin ointment can be applied to the diaper area before bedtime. Superabsorbent diapers or a double layer of diapers can retain more urine and keep the baby from becoming soaked. If the parent plans to change the baby's diaper at night, dressing him in a sleep sack provides easier access.

Nasal congestion is the premier symptom of the common cold. Babies breathe through the nose, so this symptom can prove quite bothersome. Nasal congestion at night causes the baby to sleep restlessly.

A humidifier may be helpful in increasing the moisture in the air and easing the child's breathing. It is important to clean the humidifier regularly because it can become a haven for bacteria. The infant's pediatrician may also prescribe nose drops, which can aid in clearing the nasal passages. Parents should also make sure they know how to use a bulb syringe to remove mucus from a stuffy nose.

Teething pain seems to worsen at night. One explanation is that at night, when all daytime distractions are gone, the infant really begins to focus on the pain. Various ointments sold without a prescription can soothe teething pain. Home remedies, such as offering the infant a washcloth that has been moistened and briefly left in the freezer, a hard bagel, or a teething ring to gnaw on, can also be helpful.

Pinworm infections have been associated with sleep disturbance, irritability, teeth grinding, and abdominal pain. Adult pinworms are threadlike worms, approximately half an inch long, that reside in the large intestine. At night, the pregnant females migrate to the area around the anus to lay their eggs. This is what causes the common symptoms of itching and sleeplessness. A suspected pinworm infection should be brought to the attention of the child's pediatrician. The doctor may suggest a "Scotch tape test" to confirm the diagnosis. A piece of cellophane tape is applied to the anus first thing in the morning to capture some of the eggs. The pediatrician can examine the tape under the microscope to look for eggs. Pinworm infections are easily treated with medication.

Ear infections (otitis media) are common in childhood. In this condition, pus or fluid accumulates behind the eardrum in the middle section of the ear. As the pressure builds, the child experiences pain. Pain is frequently the first symptom, and it often begins at night. The pain may even be severe enough to wake the child from sleep. Pain is related to the child's physical position. It may be especially strong during sleep because pressure on the sensitive ear structures is greatest when the child is in the prone position (face down). In addition, the ear's normal drainage mechanism, the eustachian tubes, may not work as effectively when the child is lying down.

The pediatrician needs to evaluate the child, make a definitive diagnosis, and initiate treatment. Until the child can be seen, parents may be advised to maintain the child in an upright position and administer a pain medication, such as acetaminophen.

Most instances of ear infection are unavoidable. A certain percentage of ear infections, though, are caused by putting the infant to bed with a bottle. The milk can travel up through the eustachian tubes, which connect the upper throat and the ear, and set up an infection in the middle ear. This is yet another reason to eliminate the practice of night feeding.

A number of *illnesses* can cause a child to be more sleepy than usual. These include viral infections, mononucleosis, and hepatitis. Any illness with a high fever can induce a child to sleep a greater number of hours than he would ordinarily. This change in pattern is the body's appropriate reaction to the stress of illness. More rest conserves energy and allows the healing process to be a top priority. As the child recovers, his usual sleep patterns reemerge.

Infants with *gastroesophageal reflux* (GER) may also experience sleep disruptions. In this condition, the contents of the stomach flow backward, up into the esophagus instead of proceeding down into the intestines. Symptoms include vomiting, irritability, and refusal to feed. Reflux is affected by the infant's position. The tendency to reflux is exacerbated by the lying on the back sleep position currently recommended for infants. Decisions regarding the best sleep position for an infant with GER should be made in consultation with the pediatrician.

When the condition is severe, the stomach contents can actually be breathed into the lungs. Children with this type of GER have cough, wheezing, heartburn, poor weight gain, or episodes of coughing or choking associated with feedings.

There are a variety of treatments for GER, including thickening the child's feedings, paying careful attention to his position after feedings, and medication.

Asthma is a chronic disease of the respiratory system. Children with this condition experience cough, wheezing, and difficulty breathing as a result of narrowed air passageways in the lungs. Some children with asthma have particular difficulty with breathing when they are asleep at night. In addition to the standard medical therapies, these children should have their bedrooms checked for factors that may contribute to worsening of the disease. Dust, environmental pollutants, and pets are frequently identified as culprits. The situation can be improved by placing the pillows and mattress in special cases, removing stuffed toys and rugs, cleaning curtains and linens frequently, closing the windows, and limiting a pet's access to the room.

Many *chronic illnesses* are associated with sleep disturbances. The sleep problems can come from a variety of sources. The sleep problem may be related to the illness itself. An example is poorly controlled nighttime seizures that interfere with sleep. In other cases, certain medications that the child takes can make it difficult for him to fall asleep. Anxiety about the illness, its treatment, and its prognosis can affect a child's ability to sleep. Sometimes families allow a child special privileges, such as sleeping with the parents, during the acute phase of an illness. When the child has recovered, it can be difficult to reinstitute the old rules.

Sorting out the factor or combination of factors responsible for a chronically ill child's sleep disorder is a complex task. Concerns should be voiced to the pediatrician, specialist, or case manager, who can assist the family in resolving this important issue.

A child with *neurological problems* may have difficulty falling asleep or staying asleep because of abnormalities in the brain. A full assessment should be carried out to exclude other contributing factors, such as the side effects of medication or a behavioral problem, such as inappropriate sleep onset associations. A child with a true inability to sleep may benefit from sedative medication at bedtime.

Medications can affect sleep in various ways. Medications that are known to cause sleepiness include antihistamines (used to treat allergies), anticonvulsants (used to treat seizures), and analgesics (used to treat pain). Stimulant medication used to treat attention deficit disorder and theophylline preparations prescribed for asthma are associated with insomnia. Caffeine is associated with sleeplessness as well. Antibiotics can cause either increased or decreased sleep. Bothersome side effects of medication should be discussed with the child's physician. It is possible that the child could be switched to a related preparation that would not deleteriously affect his sleep.

Part Four

SLEEP DISORDERS

26

INSOMNIA

Eight-year-old Dana was a model child. She was a top student and enjoyed many close friendships. She excelled in gymnastics and music in addition to her schoolwork. She was very compliant about getting herself ready for her 8:30 P.M. bedtime. She generally liked reading in bed or listening to a tape before she turned out the light.

This was when the problems began. Dana just could not fall asleep. She tossed and turned in her bed, looking up every once in a while to see the hands of the clock advancing steadily. The later it got, the more anxious she became. After several weeks like this, she began to feel fatigued during the daytime. Sometimes, she fell asleep when she came home from school or while she was trying to do her homework. Her parents threatened to curtail her afterschool activities. This made her feel even more upset. When dark circles developed under her eyes, Dana was brought to the pediatrician for a checkup.

Dana had insomnia. *Insomnia* is a sleep disorder characterized by a deficient quantity or quality of sleep. Insomnia is a common problem in school-aged children. It may exist by itself or in combination with other sleep problems, such as sleepwalking, sleeptalking, and night fears. This key explores some of the causes of insomnia.

Causes of Insomnia

A child who worries excessively is at risk for insomnia. Worries rise to prominence at night, when daytime activities no longer occupy the mind. Dwelling on these concerns interferes with the relaxation necessary for sleep.

School is often a focus of the child's concerns. A child who is doing poorly in school may worry about being humiliated in class if she does not understand the work. She may also be feeling the pain of disappointing or angering her parents. She may be additionally stressed by the remedial work required by parents or tutors. The stress levels may be especially high on Sunday nights before the start of the school week and on the nights before important tests.

A child who is a perfectionist may also experience insomnia. Like Dana, she may be bright and a high achiever at school. Her self-image is dependent on superiority in the school setting. She worries about failing to maintain an above-average level of performance. If she has derived attention within the family for her academic prowess, she may fear that a less than perfect grade will mean a withdrawal of love. This type of child needs to be reassured that she is valued for herself and that parental love is not contingent upon her score on the next math test.

Dana is also an example of a child who is overprogrammed. An overprogrammed child is one who pursues a job, music or art lessons, sports, or other enrichment activities in addition to school. This heavy schedule can cause a child to feel pulled in many directions and stretched to the limit. A child in this situation has difficulty at night because she can't make the transition from the frenetic pace of the day to the calm that is a necessary prelude to sleep. Cutting down on activities and

141

helping the child find a relaxing bedtime ritual are effective ways of managing this kind of problem.

Depression can cause a child to have difficulty initiating sleep. Depression is now recognized in children with increased frequency. In addition to sleep problems, symptoms of childhood depression include poor appetite, loss of energy, withdrawal from friends and activities, decreased ability to concentrate, school problems, and feelings of worthlessness and sadness. This is a serious disorder that merits prompt pediatric consultation.

Death is a prominent concern for the preschool and school-aged child. During these years, most children undergo a personal introduction to death through the loss of a family member, friend, or pet. Many phrases in common parlance juxtapose sleep and death. A child may hear that someone has "died in his sleep." She may be told that a dead person "looks like he's sleeping." She may be familiar with the concept of a pet being "put to sleep." These phrases can lead to confusion and precipitate anxieties at night. It is important to reassure a young child that sleep and death are distinct entities. Telling the child, "See you in the morning," at bedtime is a comforting reminder that she's expected to wake up the following day.

Other triggers of insomnia are transitions, such as changes in the family constellation as a result of divorce or remarriage, moving to a new house, or transferring schools.

Change is difficult to process, and much of this processing seems to take place at night. A parent can siphon off some of the nighttime anxieties by addressing anticipated changes with the child during the day. Parents may be stressed themselves by the changes, but it is critical not to overlook the child's needs. It is advisable to give a child an appropriate amount of advance notice about any changes, so that she is not overwhelmed and has a chance to adjust. The insomnia linked with transitions should be self-limited. If it lingers, other causes for the problem should be investigated.

Medication can be another cause of insomnia. The most commonly implicated drugs are the stimulant medications prescribed in the treatment of attention deficit hyperactivity disorder, theophylline preparations that are used in the treatment of asthma, and phenobarbital, which is used to treat seizure disorders. A child can also react with agitation to some of the ingredients in over-the-counter cold remedies. The child's caffeine intake after dinner should be monitored, since this may be a factor in some cases.

Insomnia occurs in childhood, particularly during the school years. A specific trigger can usually be identified. This factor should be diligently sought and addressed so that these formative years can be enjoyed to the fullest.

Follow-up

Dana had a full physical examination, which was completely normal. When she was alone with her physician, she confided that she was experiencing immense pressure about her schoolwork. She felt that her parents were never satisfied with her performance and were always pushing her to take on extra projects. She was not sure that she would be able to handle all her responsibilities at a consistently high level. Dana and her family sat down and established priorities for the various studies, clubs, teams, and choirs that occupied her time. They pared down the list, and within weeks, Dana no longer had any difficulty falling asleep.

27

NIGHT TERRORS

Chris, age four, regularly went to bed at 8 P.M. without difficulty. One night, at 10 P.M., his parents heard screams coming from Chris's room. When they arrived at the bedside, Chris was sitting up in bed and sobbing. His eyes were wide open and staring. He did not respond to his parents' attempts to comfort him. He did not even seem to recognize them. After 15 minutes, he relaxed and returned to sleep on his own. Chris seemed fine in the morning and had no memory of the event.

Mr. and Mrs. Parker were puzzled and worried about Chris's bizarre behavior. They were convinced that he was awake during the episode because he was sitting up and his eyes were open. Yet, his lack of responsiveness was unusual. Chris's parents wanted to help their son but were unsure about what to do.

What Chris experienced was a night terror. Night terrors represent an incomplete awakening from stage IV non-REM sleep. Stage IV sleep is normally very deep in young children. The depth of this type of sleep can sometimes make the transition to the next sleep cycle difficult. When this occurs, the result is a night terror. During this partial wakening, it is characteristic that features of both sleep and wakefulness are present simultaneously.

Night terrors are experienced by five percent of children. They usually occur between the ages of six months and six years, with a peak incidence at ages three to four. The tendency to have night terrors runs in families.

Anatomy of a Night Terror

Night terrors typically occur one to four hours after a child goes to sleep because this is when the bulk of stage IV sleep occurs. The child does not report a dream, because dreaming does not occur during stage IV sleep. Similarly, the child is not capable of forming a memory of the event. Since it is typical that the child has no recollection of having had a night terror, posing questions about it at the time or in the morning is unnecessary. Questioning can actually be harmful if it makes the child feel strange or embarrassed. Night terrors can take place more than once in a single night. They can even occur during a daytime nap. Night terrors can vary in frequency over time and may persist for a period of months.

Nightmare or Night Terror?

Night terrors must be differentiated from nightmares, which are described in Key 24. Nightmares are bad dreams. They tend to occur in the early morning hours rather than several hours after bedtime. A child who has had a nightmare may cry and appear frightened. His crying is a response to the scary content of the dream, not a part of the dream itself, for by this time the dream is completely over.

The child is easily aroused and comforted by parental attention. He may be able to recall the dream in detail. The child may be reluctant to return to sleep for fear that the dream will recur. He may relish his parents' company until he can relax and fall back to sleep. In the morning, he is able to recall having had a dream.

Coping with Night Terrors

Chris's parents were reassured that night terrors are not a cause for concern in children under the age of six years. They were advised that they could be present in his room during an episode but that they should not actively intervene. They should simply let the episode run its course. Mr. and Mrs. Parker expressed how helpless they felt when they were unable to do anything to assist their son. It was even more difficult for them when their comforting maneuvers were rebuffed.

Once the episode was over, Chris was expected to fall back to sleep on his own and there was no need to awaken him. There was nothing to be gained by asking Chris about the experience. Since he would be unable to remember it, questioning would only make him anxious.

Preventing Night Terrors

Night terrors are more frequent when a child is overtired. Making sure that a susceptible child gets an adequate amount of sleep is important. This is especially critical during long trips and vacations, when sleep schedules tend to become disrupted. A child who has a consistently abnormal sleep pattern is also more likely to have night terrors. A regular sleep schedule remedies this situation by ensuring a smoother transition between the various sleep stages.

Night Terrors in the Older Child

When night terrors occur in children over the age of six, psychological factors should be investigated. Night terrors in this age group may be a reflection of some stress or anxiety the child is experiencing. Often, the child is functioning well in other areas and the night terror is the only manifestation of difficulty. This is a situation in which counseling is beneficial.

28

SLEEPTALKING AND SLEEPWALKING

Peter talked in his sleep. He sat up in bed with his eyes open and he mumbled. Occasionally, he said distinct words. After a minute, he stretched, turned over, and returned to sleep.

Jody walked in his sleep. His eyes were open, but they didn't appear to be focusing in the normal way. He didn't seem to recognize his parents but could respond appropriately to simple questions like, "Are you okay?" He wandered around the house as if he were looking for something. Eventually a parent could guide him back to bed. Once, on his way back to bed, he urinated in the closet. He returned to sleep without fully waking.

Kara walked in her sleep, too. She moved about her room in a frantic and disoriented way. She did not respond to verbal or physical overtures. Sometimes, she yelled things like, "Go away" or "No, no, no." She calmed down on her own after about 20 minutes. She woke up for a short time and then went back to sleep. She never reported strange dreams the morning after a sleepwalking episode. She never had any memory of the event itself.

Over the last several months, Kara's mother had had several hospitalizations and debilitating treatments for a serious illness. Kara helped out by taking over many of the household responsibilities.

Peter, Jody, and Kara share the same underlying cause for their sleep disturbances. Sleeptalking and sleepwalking result from a partial waking from nondreaming (stage IV non-REM) sleep.

Characteristics of Partial Wakings

Stage IV sleep is very deep in young children. Sometimes, it is hard to break the hold of this deep sleep and the transition from this stage to waking does not go smoothly. When this occurs, the child is left in a state that has features of both waking and sleeping. Sleeptalking and sleepwalking are two behaviors that occur in this halfway zone.

Sleeptalking and sleepwalking usually take place one to four hours after falling asleep. This is because the bulk of deep non-REM sleep occurs during the first two sleep cycles. The child has no memory of the event because memories are not formed during non-REM sleep.

A common misconception is that a child who walks or talks in his sleep is responding to a dream. A child is not capable of these kinds of complex body movements during dreaming sleep.

Sleeptalking is reported in 50 percent of children. It is considered a normal phenomenon and does not require treatment.

It is estimated that 15 percent of children have at least one episode of sleepwalking. It occurs most frequently between three and seven years and is not considered pathological at this time. Its occurrence at these young ages is thought to reflect the child's immature sleep patterns.

If this phenomenon is present during the school years or adolescence, further investigation is warranted. In these age groups, there is usually an underlying emotional cause.

A common scenario involves a child like Kara who is under a great deal of pressure and who is struggling to control her feelings.

Emotional problems are not the only causes of sleepwalking. There are various reports that sleepwalking is precipitated by a full bladder, a heavy meal before bedtime, or certain medications, most notably methylphenidate (Ritalin). Some children are more prone to sleepwalk when they are ill and have a fever. There may be an increase in sleepwalking incidents when the child is fatigued. Night terrors and enuresis (see Key 29) occur more frequently among sleepwalkers. The tendency to sleepwalk has a familial basis. A child who sleepwalks is likely to have a parent or close relative who also exhibited this behavior.

Another important factor is the frequency of these events. A single yearly sleepwalk has very different implications for a child and family than multiple nightly episodes.

Handling Sleepwalking

The management of sleepwalking is very straightforward. The episode should be allowed to run its course. It resolves when the transition from stage IV non-REM sleep to waking has been completed. It takes some time for this process to occur. Waking the child from deep sleep is quite difficult to accomplish and is not likely to shorten the episode in any case. The end of the episode is signaled by behaviors like Peter's. They include yawning, stretching, turning over, readjusting the covers, and returning to sleep.

The safety of the sleepwalker is of paramount concern. It may be possible to lead a calm sleepwalker, like Jody, back to his room, where he is less likely to harm himself. An agitated sleepwalker, like Kara, resists physical approaches. In this situation, parents must simply watch and wait.

149

Protective changes can be made in the child's environment. The child who has a tendency to sleepwalk should not be assigned to the top bunk. Stairways or the door to the child's room can be gated so he does not have access to potentially dangerous areas of the house. Hallways should be kept free of obstacles that might pose tripping hazards. Additional locks may need to be placed high out of reach on any doors and windows that lead to the outside. Doors may also be outfitted with an alarm system. Some parents attach a bell to the door of the child's room so that they can be alerted to the time when he is up and about.

Sensitivity to the child's feelings about sleepwalking is critical. It is mortifying to find out, as Jody did, that he had urinated onto the closet floor and that the entire family had gathered to watch the sleepwalking spectacle. Asking the child about the episode in the morning is fruitless because he has no memory of it. The questioning serves only to make him feel uncomfortable and out of control.

Questioning would be particularly counterproductive in Kara's situation. She is already struggling hard during the daytime with events that are beyond her control. The added stress of worrying about her nighttime behavior may actually lead to an increased frequency of sleepwalking.

Counseling is indicated for children who sleepwalk past the age of seven. Professional assistance should also be sought for any child who sleepwalks frequently. Medications are another option in the treatment of sleepwalking. They are usually reserved, however, for the most severe cases.

29

BEDWETTING

Eight-year-old Frank never accepted an invitation to sleep over at a friend's house. He wet his bed almost every night. He was embarrassed about it and avoided all overnight visits so that his friends would not find out about his problem.

Frank's parents tried to help him by restricting the amount of liquids he was allowed to consume after dinner. They would also wake Frank at 11 P.M. before they went to bed so that he could use the bathroom.

None of these measures worked. His bed was still wet on a nightly basis. Frank was upset. His parents were angry and frustrated. They threatened to take away his video games unless he stopped wetting the bed.

Bedwetting is a common problem among young children. The medical term for bedwetting is *nocturnal enuresis*. Nocturnal enuresis can be divided into two types. *Primary* nocturnal enuresis, which applies to 70 to 75 percent of bedwetters, means that the child has never been dry at night on a consistent basis. *Secondary* enuresis is the term used when a child resumes wetting the bed after a dry period of six months. Secondary enuresis is thought to be precipitated by a psychological stress, such as an illness, a move, the birth of a sibling, or the death of a family member. Primary nocturnal enuresis is the focus of this chapter. Secondary enuresis should be referred to the child's physician.

The relationship between bedwetting and sleep is not completely understood. Some parents of children who wet their beds describe their offspring as exceptionally sound sleepers. Some parents report great difficulty in waking these children from sleep to use the bathroom at night.

These descriptions have not been documented in clinical studies, however. Sleep studies show that enuresis occurs during all phases of the sleep cycle, with no increased frequency during deep sleep. No differences have been found in the structure of sleep between enuretic children and those who are dry at night. Enuretic children do not spend more time in deep sleep. Some children recall dreaming about water only to awaken in wet sheets. It is not clear which comes first in this situation. The dream may have influenced the child to void, or perhaps lying in a wet bed caused the child to dream about water.

Various studies report that up to 22 percent of 6-year-old boys and 18 percent of 6-year-old girls have enuresis. By age 11, the incidence is 13 percent for white boys, 22 percent for black boys, 9 percent for white girls, and 12 percent for black girls. The incidence is reduced to less than 3 percent in 18 year olds.

A child's bedwetting is determined by developmental, biological, and genetic factors. It is not a behavior done on purpose or out of disobedience. Anatomic problems or treatable diseases are rarely the cause of primary nocturnal enuresis.

Up to 85 percent of children with enuresis have reduced bladder capacities even though their bladders are physically normal. They also urinate more frequently during the day. One theory is that they wet the bed because their bladders cannot retain an entire night's volume of urine.

152

Family history strongly influences the development of enuresis. If both a child's parents were enuretic, the chance of the child having the problem is 75 percent.

There are some interesting associations between personality and enuresis. Parents note that their enuretic children are highly strung and tend to lose their tempers easily. These children are afraid of the dark and find it difficult to get to sleep. It is not known whether they have an intrinsic sleep problem or they resist going to sleep because of its association with bedwetting. In school, enuretic children are less attentive and do below-average work. They are less well liked by their peers.

There are a number of options in the treatment of enuresis. It is even possible to make progress without doing anything. Achieving urinary control is a matter of development and maturation. This maturation takes longer in some children than in others. It is estimated that 10 to 15 percent of enuretic children per year achieve control without intervention.

Some families may prefer to take a more active stance. A pediatrician's guidance is helpful in sorting out all the various treatment options.

The Pediatrician's Evaluation

The pediatrician's evaluation should include a history in which she gathers information about the child's toilet-training experiences, developmental milestones, recent stressful life events, enuresis treatments previously tried, and enuresis in other family members.

The pediatrician will also want to investigate possible medical reasons for bedwetting. These are quite rare and account for only one to three percent of cases of enuresis. Urinary tract infections, sickle cell disease, diabetes, and

153

drugs that cause an increased production of urine are the most likely physical causes. They can be diagnosed by straightforward blood or urine tests.

The pediatrician must also explore the psychological state of the family. Since so many of the treatments involve behavior modification, an assessment of the family's motivation, persistence, and ability to comply is crucial. Information about the child's situation is also important. How is he coping? Does he have any direct responsibilities in regard to the bedwetting, like changing his clothes and sheets and helping with the laundry? Is he fearful about going to the bathroom at night? Is he motivated to work on the problem?

The pediatrician must also learn about the parents' perspective. Parents may be angry about the disruption and extra work that the bedwetting problem entails. They may be frustrated when progress is slow. Frustration may lead to thoughts of taking punitive action against the child.

Education is a key element of treatment. The child and family must understand the process of urination and the reasons that bedwetting occurs. It should be emphasized to the child that he is neither bad nor lazy. The child will be relieved to know that there are probably several other children in his class with the same problem. If the parents had similar problems, they may choose to share this information with the child.

Treatment Options

Practical treatments for enuresis include bladder exercises, alarm systems, and medication. Bladder-stretching exercises are useful when a small bladder capacity is the cause for enuresis. The number of ounces that the bladder should hold corresponds to the child's age in years plus 2. A target is established by asking the child to void in a measuring cup after holding the urine for as long as possible. The child should work on recognizing the feeling of a full bladder; many children with enuresis ignore this important sensation. He stretches the bladder by holding the urine past the point at which he feels maximal fullness. This feeling subsides after several minutes so that the child is not uncomfortable during this process. The child then voids in the cup and compares the quantity to the target amount. Daily progress can be displayed on a graph. Once some progress has been achieved, a challenge can be attempted. The child is then encouraged to drink a lot of fluid and see how long he can hold the urine and what quantity of urine he eventually voids. There is a 35 percent cure rate with this method.

The use of urine alarms is suggested for well-motivated children aged seven and above. In the easiest to use, such as Wet-Stop (see the last section of this book for the address of the manufacturer) a buzzer is worn on the pajama top and a sensor is placed in a pocket sewn into a pair of regular underpants. When the child voids, the urine completes a circuit and sets off the buzzer, which wakes him. He can then finish urinating in the bathroom, change any wet items, reset the alarm, and go back to sleep. This system works by conditioning the child to recognize the sensation of a full bladder. Eventually, he wakes in anticipation of the buzzer and urinates in the bathroom on his own. This process takes two to three months to develop. There is no danger to the child from wearing such a device. The cost of the instrument may be covered by medical insurance. Success rates of up to 70 percent have been reported. When the device is discontinued, there is a relapse rate of 10 to 15 percent. It is suggested in these situations that the use of the alarm be resumed.

155

Medications

There are two medications that are prescribed for the treatment of enuresis. Imipramine has its main use as an antidepressant. The way it works to stop bedwetting is unclear, although it is possible that it increases the bladder capacity. It is taken in pill form about an hour before bedtime. The response to imipramine is seen quickly, often within a week. It is effective in 40 to 70 percent of cases. When the drug is stopped, 50 percent of children begin to wet the bed again.

Many parents are reluctant to give a child medication for enuresis. They are also concerned about the side effects, which include dry mouth, drowsiness, weight gain, dizziness, difficulty concentrating, and sleep problems. Another important consideration is the security of drug storage in the home. An accidental ingestion of this drug can be fatal to a toddler. A compromise is to have imipramine on hand for special occasions. This way a child can sleep over at a friend's house without worrying about the humiliation of a bedwetting incident.

DDAVP is a substance that is related to a hormone produced by the pituitary gland in the brain. Like the natural substance, it concentrates the urine so that less of it is produced at night. It is administered via a nasal spray before bedtime. Good results have been claimed for its use in short-term studies. Remission rates are high when the drug is stopped. Side effects include nasal inflammation, nosebleeds, headaches, and abdominal pain. Its use is somewhat controversial, since physicians are cautious about employing hormonal therapy when no documented hormone deficiency is present.

Additional Treatment Options

Other classic strategies include limiting a child's fluid intake at night and waking him to go to the bathroom.

Limiting fluids alone, however, rarely solves the problem of bedwetting. If fluid limitation can be achieved without a major battle, then it is worth doing. It is certainly not the cornerstone of any enuresis program. Waking a child to void may prevent some, but not all, episodes of wetting. If the child truly has a small bladder, he may wet later in the night, anyway.

Some children fear going to the bathroom at night. A child may be scared of the sound of the toilet or the walk down a dark corridor. Providing a night-light or flashlight may solve this problem. Another option is to place a portable potty in the child's room at night.

Sticker charts can be used alone or in combination with other strategies. The child is given a sticker in the morning as a reward for a dry night. An added incentive is to offer a special treat for a sustained period of dryness. This is a good modality for children in the younger age range who may not be able to comply with some of the other regimens. A 25 percent success rate is quoted for the sticker chart method.

Hypnosis has also been tried as a treatment for enuresis. The strength of this method is its emphasis on the child's mastery of his problem. A high degree of motivation is critical. Good results and a low failure rate are reported.

Successful treatment of enuresis achieves much more than dry sheets at night. It restores the child's self-esteem and enables him to become involved in peer-related activities. It is also a source of pride to the family who was able to make a positive change by working together.

Follow-up

Frank was seen by his pediatrician, who did not find any medical cause for his problem. Frank and his family chose to use the urine alarm in conjunction with a program of bladder-stretching exercises. After three months, he was dry at night on a consistent basis. Family tensions eased considerably. After four months, Frank wanted to see how things would work out without the alarm. He wet his bed on occasion, but not nearly as frequently as before. Frank packed up the alarm and wrapped the box in fancy paper. He is planning to give it to his brother, Simon, as a present for his seventh birthday.

30

SLEEP APNEA

Alexander's parents did not have to go to his bedside to check on him at night. His snoring was so loud that it could be heard in every corner of the house. Snoring was only part of the problem. Alexander appeared to have great difficulty breathing at night. He breathed with such effort that his chest caved in with every breath. He made gasping and snorting noises. His mouth was wide open. Occasionally, there were silent periods when he did not seem to be breathing at all. He moved around restlessly in his sleep as if he were looking for a comfortable position. Sometimes he even slept sitting up. When he had a cold, things were even worse and Mr. and Mrs. Setzen spent many anxious nights at his bedside.

This is a classic description of obstructive sleep apnea. *Apnea* is a medical term that means a stoppage of breathing. In this condition, the child stops breathing periodically during sleep because the air passageway is blocked.

How Apnea Occurs

The airway becomes blocked when the walls of the throat cave in. The place that becomes blocked is located in the back of the throat behind the base of the tongue. The walls of the throat are somewhat floppy in this area. They can collapse in on themselves when the child makes a very strong effort to breathe. Another way a blockage can occur is if the tongue flops back and covers the airway.

159

Enlarged tonsils and adenoids are also sometimes implicated in obstructive sleep apnea. The tonsils are infection-fighting lymph tissue located in the back of the mouth. These are the structures that become red and swollen when a person has a sore throat. After an infection, they can either remain enlarged or shrink to their previous size.

Adenoids are the same kind of tissue as the tonsils. Their location, in the back of the throat above the roof of the mouth, precludes their being seen directly without the benefit of special instruments. Enlarged adenoids can be suspected if the child breathes through his mouth or has a constant runny nose or *hyponasal speech* (the child cannot say "Mickey Mouse" clearly).

Enlarged tonsils and adenoids narrow the caliber of the breathing passages. When the child tries to breathe through these narrowed passageways, he must expend a greater effort to move the quantity of air he needs. This increased force of breathing can cause the floppy area in the back of the throat to cave in and block the airway.

The incidence of obstructive sleep apnea is not known. There are probably more cases now than there were a generation ago, when tonsillectomy was a routinely performed treatment for throat infection. The diagnosis can be difficult to make because the child usually looks fine in the pediatrician's office during the daytime. When the child is awake, the nerves and muscles hold the throat open and the tongue forward. The problems occur during sleep, when muscles in the region are less well coordinated.

The Significance of Snoring

An important clue that is frequently overlooked is the phenomenon of loud snoring during sleep. This may just be taken for granted as an unpleasant but inconsequential

160

family trait. As Mrs. Setzen remarked, "He sounds just like his father."

Alexander's snoring, however, was very significant. When he had periods of noisy breathing, this meant that at least some air was moving through the passageways. The silent periods corresponded to times when there was no air movement at all. This resulted in low oxygen levels in the blood. The low oxygen levels then caused him to arouse briefly and adjust the position of his throat and tongue. The loud snorts indicated that air had begun to pass once more.

Sleep Behavior

Children like Alexander are restless sleepers because they constantly shift around trying to find a position in which their airway is maximally open. Some lie on their backs with their necks extended. Others sleep sitting up or leaning forward on their knees. They do not have a good quality of sleep because of the hundreds of disruptions caused by the apneas and arousals. Their throats may be dry from the mouth breathing. They wake frequently, asking for drinks of water. Some parents reluctantly end up with the children in their bed at night because it is the easiest way to cope with the frequent night wakings.

The sleep problems can lead to behavior problems. Children with obstructive sleep apnea can be cranky and tired during the daytime. They can appear extremely active, which is actually overcompensation for fatigue. Fatigue causes them to be inattentive and do poorly in school. They may not have as much stamina as their peers for athletic pursuits. They may also wet the bed at night. (See Key 29 for more on bedwetting.)

Associations with Sleep Apnea

Other medical problems are associated with sleep apnea. Low oxygen levels can strain the heart and lungs.

161

High blood pressure and headaches can occur. Some of these children have a constant cough at night because of their difficulty in handling the normal secretions produced in the throat. Chronic mouth breathers have a higher incidence of colds and dental problems. Children with chronic obstruction may find it difficult to eat and breathe simultaneously. The obstruction may also affect their ability to smell and taste food. These factors can combine to produce a child with feeding problems and poor physical growth.

Obstructive sleep apnea can occur in any child. Certain groups of children are at particular risk of developing this condition. These include children with malformations of the nose, mouth, or throat, small jaws, large tongues, or floppy muscles. Children who have had surgery in this area, such as a cleft palate repair, should also be watched carefully. Although enlarged tonsils and adenoids are the most common cause of obstructive sleep apnea, not every child with big tonsils has this problem.

The Pediatrician's Evaluation

Parents who suspect that their child might have obstructive sleep apnea should discuss this with the pediatrician. Parents should make sure to mention the snoring, the child's breathing efforts, any periods of apnea noted, his sleeping position, night wakings, and any behavioral changes they have observed. A tape recording of the child's breathing during sleep helps the physician to recognize any periods of apnea. The diagnosis can also be made by monitoring the child's breathing in a sleep laboratory.

If sleep apnea is confirmed, the next step is to identify its cause. A careful physical examination is key to the diagnosis of malformations of the head and neck. Most obstructive apneas are caused by enlarged tonsils and adenoids. Tonsillar size can be assessed directly. Because of their location, more specialized techniques are necessary to determine the size of the adenoids. This can be done by obtaining a side-view x-ray of the neck. The drawback to this approach is that it is not always definitive. Another method involves passing a small flexible tube into the nose and looking at the adenoids directly. This procedure, called *nasopharyngoscopy* , can be done in the office, with the child awake, by a physician specializing in diseases of the ear, nose, and throat.

The treatment for obstructive sleep apnea caused by enlarged tonsils and adenoids is surgical removal. The child's pediatrician will be able to suggest appropriate remedies for apnea caused by other conditions.

Follow-up

Alexander was evaluated by an ear, nose, and throat doctor, who confirmed the diagnosis of obstructive sleep apnea due to enlarged tonsils and adenoids. Surgery was recommended. Alexander had his surgery, and within two days he stopped snoring. He no longer tossed and turned in his sleep, and his respirations were regular and effortless. Mr. and Mrs. Setzen are still at the bedside, though, because they have to get that close to hear his breathing.

QUESTIONS AND ANSWERS

How common are sleep problems?

Of all children under the age of five, 20 to 30 percent have sleep problems.

My 2½ year old does not sleep through the night. Did I do something wrong as a parent?

Most parents of children with sleep problems are loving, responsive, and concerned to a fault. It is their sensitivity and devotion to their children that sometimes impedes their ability to set appropriate limits for nighttime behavior. Sleep problems can be solved. Parental motivation, strength, and determination are key ingredients for a successful outcome.

I've stopped letting my two year old take a nap so he will sleep through the night. Is this a good idea?

Most two year olds still require a 90-minute daily nap. Overtired children do not sleep well, and their sleep is subject to frequent awakenings. It might be better to look into why he is not yet sleeping through the night and treat the problem directly.

My husband and I recently separated. How will this affect my child's sleep?

Any stress, such as a separation, divorce, move, hospitalization, serious illness, birth of a sibling, or entry into day-care, can affect a child's sleep. The most common manifestations of stress-induced sleep problems are night-time fears, inability to fall asleep, nightmares, and frequent night wakings.

My wife and I both work long hours. How can we arrange our son's sleep schedule so that we can spend time with him when we get home and still allow him to get enough sleep?

With a younger child, this situation is easily handled by manipulating his schedule so that he goes to bed later and wakes later in the morning as well. When a child must conform to regular school hours, this is more difficult. Revving the child up after dinner will surely interfere with his ability to relax and go to sleep on time. A better option is to rise a little earlier in the morning and spend some time together then. This a great way to start the day.

What is the significance of snoring?

Loud snoring accompanied by gasps, snorts, restless movements, breathing difficulties, and respiratory pauses is consistent with a diagnosis of obstructive sleep apnea. Children with this condition stop breathing periodically at night because the airway is blocked. Loud snoring in children should be brought to the attention of a physician, who can initiate an appropriate examination.

My child is in day-care and takes a long afternoon nap. How can I get her to go to sleep at a reasonable hour?

The best approach is to work this out with the day-care staff. Share your concerns with them. Perhaps they could pare half an hour from her afternoon nap, leaving her sufficiently well rested to happily finish the day but ready to sleep at her bedtime.

My eight-year-old son still wets the bed at night. He is a very sound sleeper. Is this what is causing the problem?

Many parents report that their children who bedwet also sleep very deeply. Bedwetting has been found to occur during all phases of the sleep cycle—during both deep sleep and light sleep. No differences have been found in the amount of deep sleep when children who wet the bed were compared with children who did not.

When I go in to check on my child before I go to sleep for the night, I sometimes see her moving around. I've even seen her sit up and open her eyes. Does this mean that there's something wrong?

What you have described is the behavior of a child having a partial waking at the end of non-REM sleep. A child may sit up, open her eyes and stare blankly, make chewing movements, cry out, or mumble unintelligibly. All these behaviors are normal.

My baby sleeps during the day and is up at night. How can I get her to reverse her sleep patterns?

You can remedy this situation by emphasizing the differences between daytime and nighttime caretaking. A bedtime ritual should be developed. She should be put to sleep in a consistent place. Nighttime caretaking should be low-key and businesslike. During the daytime, when she is awake, she should be provided with plenty of stimulation. Parents should gradually decrease the duration of daytime sleep until it reaches an appropriate nap length for the baby's age.

I nurse my 15-month-old daughter to sleep at night. She then gets up many times during the night and nursing is the only thing that comforts her. Help! I'm tired! What can I do to stop this?

Your daughter associates nursing with falling asleep. When she wakes up at night, as children normally do, she can't fall back to sleep unless she is nursing. She needs to learn how to fall asleep on her own so that she can settle herself back down after waking at night. If you want to continue to nurse her at night, make sure that the last nursing is sufficiently distant from the time she goes to bed so that it is no longer part of her associations with sleep.

To deal with a sleep problem, will I have to let my child cry it out?

No. There are graduated approaches to dealing with sleep problems that are kinder to the child and to the parents. Any change in the sleep routine is likely to be viewed negatively by the child, however. Crying is therefore expected. The short-term crying associated with changing a child's sleep behavior does not lead to emotional difficulties.

Is it selfish of me to want my child to sleep through the night so that I can get a full night's sleep as well?

Absolutely not. Parenting is hard work even when one is well rested, and it is vastly more difficult when one is exhausted. Parents who want to sleep at night recognize this. Well-rested parents are more energetic and more patient. They are more capable of living up to their potential as parents. This can only be beneficial to the child.

My child grinds his teeth during sleep. What is the significance of this behavior?

Up to 15 percent of normal children grind their teeth during sleep. The grinding is the result of muscular activity of the jaw muscles. Teeth grinding is also sometimes associated with tension. Grinding may cause dental problems.

What can I do to avoid sleep problems in the future?

A good bedtime ritual sets the stage for sleep in a positive way. Another key piece of advice is to set the child down awake in the place where he is expected to spend the night. If the child learns to settle himself at bedtime, he will also be able to settle himself after spontaneous wakings at night.

GLOSSARY

Adenoids   infection-fighting tissue located in the back of the throat above the roof of the mouth.

Airway   passage for air that extends from the back of the throat to the lungs.

Analgesics   medications used to treat pain.

Anticonvulsants   medications used to treat seizures.

Antihistamines   medications used to treat allergies.

Apnea   stoppage of breathing.

Bedtime ritual   a series of calming activities used to set the stage for sleep.

Bladder   the body organ that stores urine.

Cosleeping   custom of parents and children sleeping together.

Enuresis   the involuntary passage of urine during the night.

Eustachian tubes   passage between the middle ear and the upper throat that serves as a drainage system for the middle ear.

Gastroesophageal reflux   a condition in which the stomach contents flow up into the esophagus rather than down into the intestines.

Hepatitis   an infection of the liver.

Hyponasal voice   a voice disorder associated with increased adenoidal tissue.

Insomnia   sleep disorder characterized by deficient quality or quantity of sleep.

Methylphenidate   (Ritalin) a medication used to treat attention deficit hyperactivity disorder.

Mononucleosis   a generalized infection caused by the Epstein-Barr virus.

Nasopharyngoscopy   a diagnostic procedure involving the passage of a flexible tube through the nose, used to evaluate the adenoids and palate.

Nightmare   a bad dream usually brought on by a frightening or stressful daytime event.

Night terror   partial awakening from non-REM sleep characterized by a frightened-looking and unresponsive child.

Non-REM sleep   (non-rapid eye movement) a normally occurring deep sleep state, associated with night terrors, sleepwalking, and sleeptalking.

Obstructive sleep apnea   stoppage of breathing during sleep because of a blockage in the air passageway.

Otitis media   infection of the middle ear.

Pinworm   parasitic infection associated with anal itching and sleeplessness.

REM sleep   (rapid eye movement) a light sleep state during which dreaming occurs.

Rhythmic behaviors   headbanging, body rocking, and head rolling.

Sleep cycle   the time interval between two consecutive appearances of the same sleep state.

Sleep onset associations   conditions under which an individual becomes used to falling asleep.

Stage IV sleep   the deepest stage of non-REM sleep.

Stimulant medication   the class of medications used to treat attention deficit hyperactivity disorder.

Theophylline   a medication used in the treatment of asthma.

Tonsils   infection-fighting tissue located in the back of the throat.

Transitional object   a special soft toy or blanket a child uses for self-comforting.

RESOURCES

American Sleep Disorders Association National Office
1610 Fourteenth Street N.W., Suite 300
Rochester, MN 55901
(507) 287-6006

Can provide a listing of accredited sleep centers.

Association of Sleep Disorders Centers
P.O. Box 2604
Del Mar, CA 92014

Can provide names of sleep centers.

National Center on Child Abuse and Neglect
Department of Health and Human Services
P.O. Box 1182
Washington, DC 20013
(202) 245-0586

Provides information for parents.

National Committee for Prevention of Child Abuse
Prevent Child Abuse
P.O. Box 2866
Chicago, IL 60690
(312) 663-3520

Prevention-oriented group that can provide parenting information.

National Enuresis Society
8901 West Golf Road, Suite 303
Des Plaines, IL 60016

Support and information concerning enuresis.

Parents Anonymous
520 South Lafayette Park Place, Suite 316
Los Angeles, CA 90057
(800) 421-0353

Self-help group for parents under stress.

RECOMMENDED BOOKS AND MUSIC FOR CHILDREN

Books for Infants

Goodnight Moon   Margaret Wise Brown
      A classic pairing of text and illustrations that sets the standard for soothing going-to-bed books. (The book is also available in board-book format. Devoted fans can now purchase a stuffed version of the little bunny.)

The Baby's Bedtime Book   Kay Chorao
      A collection of poems and lullabies. (An audio version, sung by Judy Collins, is also available; see Lullaby Tapes.)

Family   Say Goodnight   Helen Oxenbury
      Appealing portrayals of family life.

Books for Toddlers

Each Peach Pear Plum   Janet and Allan Ahlberg
      Simple rhyming text and hidden fairy-tale characters combine in this delightful and innovative book.

Ten, Nine, Eight   Molly Bang
      A warm father and daughter getting-ready-for-bed book that doubles as a counting book.

The Little Fur Family   Margaret Wise Brown
A sweet book in which the loving fur family goes through its daily activities, including bedtime. The book is even covered in fake fur!

Maisy Goes to Bed   Lucy Collins
Children can help Maisy get a drink, go to the potty, and brush her teeth (courtesy of push-and-pull tabs) as she readies herself for bed.

I Am a Little Rabbit   Francois Crozat
The little rabbit narrates the story of his day; stunning color illustrations.

When I'm Sleepy   Jane R. Howard
A little girl wonders what it would be like to sleep the way various animals do.

Twinkle Twinkle Little Star   Jannat Messenger
An ingenious book in which the song plays (thanks to a microchip) as the sky darkens and a child is tucked into bed.

How Many Kisses Goodnight   Jean Monrad
A soothing rendition of a mother-daughter bedtime ritual.

Once a Lullaby   bp Nichol
A series of animals, a boy, and a girl go to sleep. The rhythmic text is like a lullaby and the music is actually provided. The illustrations are beautiful and richly detailed.

The Bed Book   Sylvia Plath
A poetic introduction to some very unusual beds.

Max's Bedtime   Rosemary Wells
   Max has to have everything right in place before he can go to bed. Children will readily identify with Max's situation.

The Napping House   Audrey and Don Wood
   A humorous tale of creatures piling on the bed for a rest with a surprise ending. The rhythmic cadence of the text and the lovely illustrations are soothing.

Books for Preschoolers

Grandfather Twilight   Barbara Berger
   A soothing and magical story about the moonrise.

The Very Quiet Cricket   Eric Carle
   Not a bona fide bedtime book, but the rhythmic text, glorious illustrations, and surprise ending make this a comforting end-of-the-day story.

Miss Rumphius   Barbara Cooney
   What better-end-of-the-day thought than the admonition to do something to make the world more beautiful?

Tucking Mommy In   Morag Loh
   A warm and lovely role reversal story in which the daughters tuck in their exhausted mother.

Where Did You Put Your Sleep?   M. Newfield
   A girl has difficulty getting to sleep until her father helps her out.

Night Is Coming   W. Nikola-Lisa
   Calm feelings are generated for the reader as day draws to a close on a picturesque farm.

In the Night Kitchen   Maurice Sendak
Mickey helps the bakers prepare the morning cake; a classic.

The Sandman   Robert Shepperson
Jay and the Sandman have a fun-filled night together.

Ira Sleeps Over   Bernard Waber
Ira is in a quandry about whether to bring his teddy bear along on his first sleep-over.

The Sleepytime Book   Jan Wahl
Animals settle for the night in lulling verse.

Books for School-aged Children

Ten in a Bed   Allan Ahlberg and Andre Amstutz
A little girl tells vaguely familiar bedtime stories to a cast of fairy-tale characters.

When the Dark Comes Dancing: A Bedtime Poetry Book   Nancy Larrick
A collection of lullabies and poems.

Fables   Arnold Lobel
This collection of fables, each with its own moral, will provoke some thoughtful end-of-the-day discussions.

Owl Moon   Jane Yolen
An evocative story of closeness between father and child.

Books about Fears, Dreams, and Nightmares

Ben's Dream   Chris Van Allsburg
Ben has a dream prompted by his reading of a geography book.

The Bad Dream   Jim Aylesworth
    A story that provides comfort for children who have experienced nightmares (preschool).

Harry and the Terrible Whatzit   Dick Gackenbach
    A dealing-with-monsters story (toddler, preschool).

Bedtime for Frances   Russell Hoban
    Frances's parents provide her with reassurance about her nighttime fears (preschool).

There's a Nightmare in My Closet   Mercer Mayer
    A boy discovers that his nightmare is not so scary after all (preschool).

Thundercake   Patricia Polacco
    A resourceful grandmother's recipe for dealing with her granddaughter's fear of storms (preschool, school-age).

My Mama Says There Aren't Any Zombies, Ghosts, Vampires, Creatures, Demons, Monsters, Fiends, Goblins, or Things   Judith Viorst
    But a little boy isn't so sure (preschool).

Lullaby Tapes

The Baby's Bedtime Book   Kay Chorao
    Judy Collins sings the verses.

Lullabies Go Jazz   Crosse, Fischer, Smith, Conte
    Expand the child's musical horizons.

Lullabies from Around the World   Steve Bergman
    Orchestra plus flute, heartbeat, and nature sounds.

Other Sources for Music

Chinaberry Book Service
2780 Via Orange Way
Spring Valley, CA 92078
(800) 776-2242

Music for Little People
P.O. Box 1460
Redway, CA 95560
(800) 346-4445

Imagery Tapes

Goodnight   Jim Weiss
A tape with six vignettes of suitable-for-bedtime guided imagery with soothing music (ages 2½–8).

Imagine Yourself to Sleep, Volumes I and II
Hand in Hand Catalog
(800) 872-9745
Children are asked to imagine that they are various animals (ages 4–10).

Starbright   Maureen Garth
A collection of 10 vignettes that can launch a child to sleep with pleasant thought (ages 3–8).

Sweet Dreams for Little Ones   Michael Pappas
Vignettes that deal with such themes as affection and responsibility, with the child in the central role (ages 4–7).

Other Devices

SleepTight Infant Soother
(800) NO-COLIC
Device that attaches to crib and simulates the experience of a car ride.

Wet-Stop
Palco Labs
5026 Scotts Valley Drive
Scotts Valley, CA 95066
    Bedwetting alarm system.

Crib tent
Right Start Catalog
(800) 548-8531

INDEX